CONTENTS

INTRODUCTION

My favorite things are old with a bit of wear, items with a history. This obsession began when I was a child and would spend my days with my grandmother, who was a seamstress. She kept an old Prince Albert tobacco tin filled with vintage buttons that provided me hours of enjoyment. Stacks of old feedsack quilt tops filled her closet, and she saved old pieces of lace, trims, and every scrap of fabric. I learned from her that beautiful things could be made from those old leftover bits. Always busy stitching, she passed her love of handwork on to me.

When you make a quilt, you stitch a piece of your life into it and the things that make up your history often find their way into your choices. You can see the influence of the years spent with my grandmother in most of my quilts. They tend to have a vintage look. I favor soft, muted colors, florals mixed with woven plaids and stripes that create a timeworn look. Handwork in the form of appliqué, embroidery, and quilting is a constant for me. I stitch through sorrow and happiness.

I'm strongly influenced by antique quilts in both design and style. I favor a folk-art, make-do style, and I make all my own samples for my books. When I'm stitching, I love to binge-watch British television programs. You'll find this passion has made its way into my quilts—or at least their names. Many of my quilts are named for English villages. I like to think that these quilts would look perfect in an old stone cottage, draped over a sofa by the fire: vintage, with a touch of romance. I hope you enjoy creating the quilts and projects in this book. Savor the journey of making each project and stitching your story.

~Dawn

Named for a charming village in Cornwall, Padstow is pieced from just six different blocks. However, using various colors and mixing up the value placement make it look like there are many more unique blocks. Dig into your scrap basket to create a charming quilt, reminiscent of times gone by.

◆

Materials

Yardage is based on 42"-wide fabric. This quilt is very scrappy, so the yardage is approximate. The prints will be used in blocks in random placement.

2½ yards *total* of assorted brown prints for blocks and binding

1½ yards *total* of assorted red prints for blocks

2 yards *total* of assorted cream/tan prints for blocks

1⅝ yards *total* of assorted blue prints for blocks

⅜ yard *total* of assorted green prints for blocks

½ yard *total* of assorted gold prints for blocks

¼ yard *total* of assorted gray prints for blocks

⅛ yard of orange print for blocks

½ yard of pink print for blocks and binding

6¾ yards of fabric for backing

81" × 90" piece of batting

Cutting for Binding

Refer to the quilt photo on page 8 and the assembly diagram on page 13 for fabric and color inspiration. Cutting information for the six block designs is included with each set of block instructions. All measurements include ¼" seam allowances.

From *each* of the brown and pink prints, cut:
- 4 strips, 2¼" × 42" (8 total)

16 Patch Blocks

Make eight blocks.

CUTTING

From the assorted prints for blocks, cut a *total* of:
- 128 squares, 2¾" × 2¾"

MAKING THE BLOCKS

Press all seam allowances as indicated by the arrows.

1 Choose 16 squares in color combinations that suit you for each block. Make eight stacks of 16 squares each.

FINISHED QUILT: 72½" × 81½"
FINISHED BLOCK: 9" × 9"

Pieced and quilted by Dawn Heese

Plain & Fancy Quilts

2 Lay out 16 squares in four rows of four squares each. Sew the squares into rows and then join the rows to make a 16 Patch block. Make eight blocks measuring 9½" square, including seam allowances.

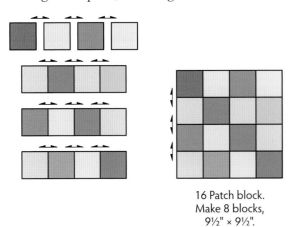

16 Patch block.
Make 8 blocks,
9½" × 9½".

3 Sew a 2" × 5¾" strip to the left side of the four-patch unit. Sew a 1¼" × 7¼" strip to the bottom to make a unit measuring 6½" × 7¼", including seam allowances.

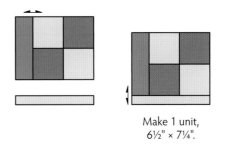

Make 1 unit,
6½" × 7¼".

4 Sew a 2¾" × 6½" strip to the right side of the unit from step 3. Sew 2" × 9½" strips to the top and bottom of the unit to make a Four Patch Cabin block. Make five blocks measuring 9½" square, including seam allowances.

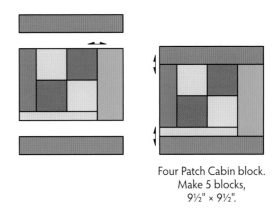

Four Patch Cabin block.
Make 5 blocks,
9½" × 9½".

Four Patch Cabin Blocks

Make five blocks.

CUTTING

From the assorted prints for blocks, cut a *total* of:
- 20 squares, 3⅛" × 3⅛"
- 5 strips, 2¾" × 6½"
- 10 strips, 2" × 9½"
- 5 strips, 2" × 5¾"
- 5 strips, 1¼" × 7¼"

MAKING THE BLOCKS

1 Select one set of the following pieces for each of the five blocks. For each block you'll need four 3⅛" squares, one 2¾" × 6½" strip, two 2" × 9½" strips, one 2" × 5¾" strip, and one 1¼" × 7¼" strip.

2 Join four 3⅛" squares to make a four-patch unit measuring 5¾" square, including seam allowances.

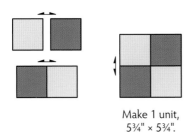

Make 1 unit,
5¾" × 5¾".

Arbor Window Blocks

The look of this block varies greatly depending on fabric placement, so have fun and mix it up! Make 27 blocks.

CUTTING

From the assorted prints, cut a *total* of:
- 54 squares, 4¼" × 4¼"; cut the squares into quarters diagonally to yield 216 side triangles
- 54 squares, 2⅜" × 2⅜"; cut the squares in half diagonally to yield 108 corner triangles
- 351 squares, 2⅝" × 2⅝"

MAKING THE BLOCKS

1 For each block, choose four corner triangles, eight side triangles, and 13 squares in a color combination you like. Stack the pieces for each block together; make 27 stacks. I find it's best to sort the pieces before sewing them to be sure I'm not left with combinations I don't love toward the end of making the blocks.

2 Lay out all the pieces for one block. Sew the pieces into diagonal rows and then join the rows to make an Arbor Window block. Make 27 blocks measuring 9½" square, including seam allowances.

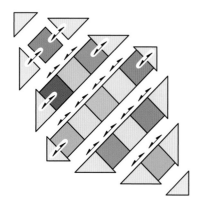

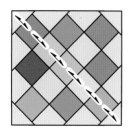

Arbor Window block
Make 27 blocks, 9½" × 9½".

Nine Patch Blocks

Make 19 blocks.

CUTTING

From the assorted prints, cut a *total* of:
- 171 squares, 3½" × 3½"

MAKING THE BLOCKS

1 Sort the squares into stacks of nine squares for each block in color combinations that suit you. You can use just two colors or multiple colors per block. Make a total of 19 stacks.

2 Lay out the squares from one stack in three rows of three squares each. Sew the squares into rows and then join the rows to make a Nine Patch block. Make 19 blocks measuring 9½" square, including seam allowances.

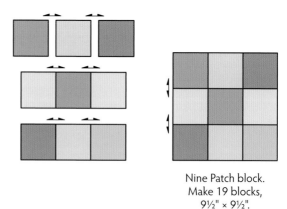

Nine Patch block.
Make 19 blocks,
9½" × 9½".

Nine Patch Cross Blocks

Make four blocks.

CUTTING

From the assorted prints, cut a *total* of:
- 16 squares, 3½" × 3½"
- 48 strips, 1½" × 3½"
- 36 squares, 1½" × 1½"

MAKING THE BLOCKS

1 For each block, you'll need nine 1½" squares, four 3½" squares, and 12 strips. Sort through your pieces and make a stack for each of the four blocks in color combinations that suit you.

2 Join the nine 1½" squares to create a nine-patch unit measuring 3½" square, including seam allowances.

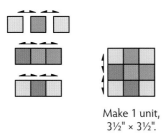

Make 1 unit,
3½" × 3½".

3 Join three 1½" × 3½" strips to make a strip unit. Make four units measuring 3½" square, including seam allowances.

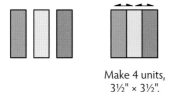

Make 4 units,
3½" × 3½".

4 Join the four strip units, the nine-patch unit, and four 3½" squares to make a Nine Patch Cross block. Make four blocks measuring 9½" square, including seam allowances.

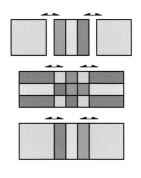
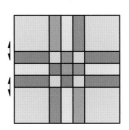

Nine Patch Cross block.
Make 4 blocks,
9½" × 9½".

Nine Patch-in-a-Square Block

Make nine blocks.

CUTTING

From the assorted prints, cut a *total* of:

- 18 squares, 5½" × 5½"; cut the squares in half diagonally to yield 36 triangles (I used matching pairs of squares so that all the triangles in a block matched.)
- 81 squares, 2⅝" × 2⅝"

MAKING THE BLOCKS

1 For each block, you'll need nine squares and four triangles. Sort through your pieces and make a stack for each of the nine blocks in color combinations that suit you.

2 Lay out the nine squares in three rows of three squares each. Sew the squares into rows and then join the rows to make a nine-patch unit measuring 6⅞" square, including seam allowances.

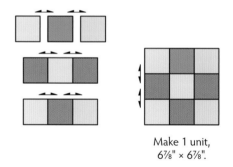

Make 1 unit,
6⅞" × 6⅞".

3 Center and sew triangles to opposite sides of the nine-patch unit. Center and sew triangles to the remaining two sides of the unit to make a Nine Patch-in-a-Square block. Make nine blocks and trim them to 9½" square, including seam allowances.

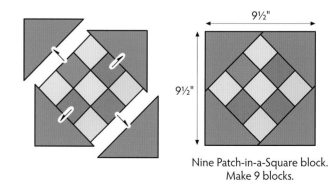

Nine Patch-in-a-Square block.
Make 9 blocks.

Assembling the Quilt Top

Referring to the quilt assembly diagram below, lay out the blocks in nine rows of eight blocks each. Sew the blocks into rows and then join the rows to make the quilt center. Your block colors may not be the same as the diagram, but block placement is important to create the same look as the original. The quilt top should measure 72½" × 81½".

Finishing the Quilt

For more details on any finishing steps, visit ShopMartingale.com/HowtoQuilt for free downloadable information.

1 Layer the quilt top with batting and backing; baste the layers together.

2 Quilt by hand or machine. The quilt shown is hand quilted with straight lines running either diagonally or horizontally and vertically through each block. This is a simple style of quilting that fits the look of yesteryear that I wanted to achieve.

3 Use the pink and brown 2¼"-wide strips to make scrappy double-fold binding. Attach the binding to the quilt.

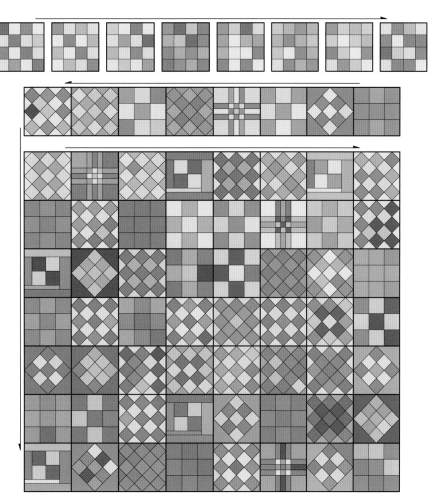

Quilt assembly

Padstow

Who says folk art can't also be romantic? My variation
of the traditional Coxcombs and Currants block is very folksy.
I love the fun and funky fernlike leaves that form the wreath
around the coxcombs, and the beauty of them is that they
don't require perfect placement. The subtle polka dot
background adds to the circular movement of the design.

Materials

Yardage is based on 42"-wide fabric.

3⅛ yards of cream dot for appliqué background

1¾ yards *total* of assorted green prints and plaids for
leaves, calyxes, and stems

1¾ yards of taupe check for small leaves, outer border,
and binding

¾ yard *total* of burgundy prints for berries, flowers,
buds, and medium and small circles

⅛ yard *total* of pink prints for flowers

⅛ yard of yellow print for flowers and large circles

⅓ yard of yellow plaid for inner border

4 yards of fabric for backing

70" × 70" piece of batting

Seam sealant, such as Fray Block

Freezer paper

½" bias-tape maker

Perfect Circles appliqué templates by Karen Kay
Buckley (optional)

Water-soluble marker or chalk pencil

String

Cutting

All measurements include ¼" seam allowances.

From the cream dot, cut:
- 4 squares, 25½" × 25½"

From the assorted green prints and plaids, cut:
- 4 strips, 1" × 11½"

**From the remainder of the assorted green prints
and plaids, cut *on the bias*:**
- 8 strips, 1" × 7"

From the taupe check, cut:
- 6 strips, 6" × 42"
- 7 strips, 2¼" × 42"

From the yellow plaid, cut:
- 6 strips, 1½" × 42"

FINISHED QUILT: 63½" × 63½"
FINISHED BLOCK: 25" × 25"

———— ◆ ————

*Appliquéd and pieced by Dawn Heese;
quilted by Hawthorne Custom Quilts*

Plain & Fancy Quilts

Appliquéing the Blocks

Refer to "Appliqué Techniques" on page 91 as needed for more details.

1 Seal the edges of each cream dot square using a seam sealant to prevent raveling and distortion during the appliqué process.

2 Using the patterns on pages 20 and 21 and pattern sheet 2, trace the shapes the indicated number of times onto the dull, nonwaxy side of the freezer paper. Cut out the shapes on the traced line to make freezer-paper templates. Cut the number of pieces noted on the patterns from the fabrics indicated. Use your favorite method to prepare the shapes for appliqué. I used Karen Kay Buckley's Perfect Circles templates to prepare the berries. See "Creating Perfect Circles," right.

3 Fold a cream dot square in half vertically and then horizontally; finger-press to establish centering lines. Tie the ends of a length of string to two water-soluble markers or chalk pencils so that the markers are 9¾" apart. Using the centering lines as a guide, place the tip of one pencil in the center of a cream dot square. Keeping the string fully extended, draw a circle to make a guide for the wreath portion of the block.

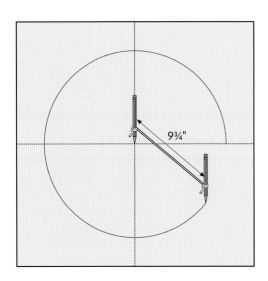

9¾"

4 Using the photo on page 16 and the drawn circle as a guide, position the fern leaves on the marked line with the center of the leaves on the line. Center the middle row of berries in each cluster on the drawn line. Then position the remaining berries. Pin or baste the pieces in place.

CREATING PERFECT CIRCLES

While this quilt has a bit of a folk-art flair so your berries and circles don't all need to be perfect, I use Perfect Circles templates by Karen Kay Buckley to prepare fabric circles for appliqué. The package comes with assorted sizes of circle templates made of heat-resistant plastic that can be reused again and again. Visit www.KarenKayBuckley.com to see videos showing how Karen makes perfectly round circles that can be stitched by hand or machine.

5 Using the bias-tape maker and the green 1"-wide strips, prepare four ½" × 11½" stems and eight ½" × 7" stems for appliqué.

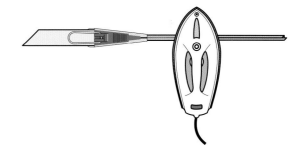

Abbey

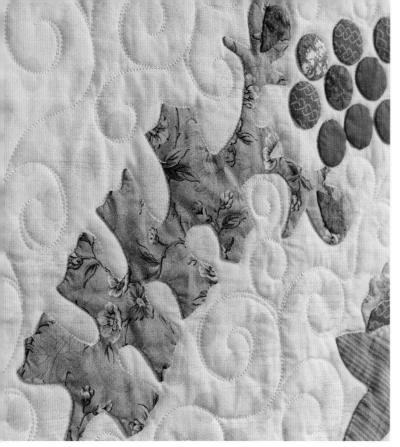

6 Position an 11½"-long stem in the center of each wreath with the bottom of the stem approximately ½" above the berries. Position the large circle approximately 1¾" from the bottom of the center stem. Add the 7"-long stems and tuck the ends under the circle. Layer flowers A–C in the center of the wreath, starting with flower A, and then add a calyx and a small circle to each flower. Pin or baste in place.

7 Hand appliqué the shapes to the background or use your favorite method. Repeat to make four blocks measuring 25½" square, including seam allowances.

Assembling the Quilt Top

Press seam allowances in the directions indicated by the arrows.

1 Referring to the quilt assembly diagram on page 19, lay out the blocks in two rows of two blocks each. Sew the blocks into rows and then join the rows. The quilt center should measure 50½" square, including seam allowances.

2 Join the yellow 1½"-wide strips end to end. From the pieced strips, cut two 52½"-long strips and two 50½"-long strips. Sew the shorter strips to the left and right sides of the quilt center. Sew the longer strips to the top and bottom edges. The quilt top should measure 52½" square, including seam allowances.

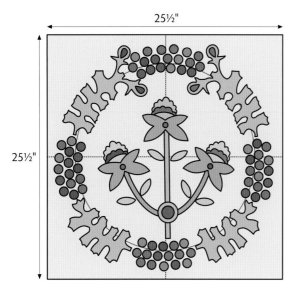

25½"

25½"

Appliqué placement

3 Join the taupe 6"-wide strips end to end. From the pieced strip, cut two 63½"-long strips and two 52½"-long strips. Sew the shorter strips to the left and right sides of the quilt. Sew the longer strips to the top and bottom edges. The quilt top should measure 63½" square.

Finishing the Quilt

For more details on any finishing steps, visit ShopMartingale.com/HowtoQuilt for free downloadable information.

1 Layer the quilt top with batting and backing; baste the layers together.

2 Quilt by hand or machine. The quilt shown is machine quilted with a swirl design in the block backgrounds and border. The wreaths, leaves, and stems are outline quilted.

3 Use the taupe 2¼"-wide strips to make double-fold binding. Attach the binding to the quilt.

Quilt assembly

Abbey

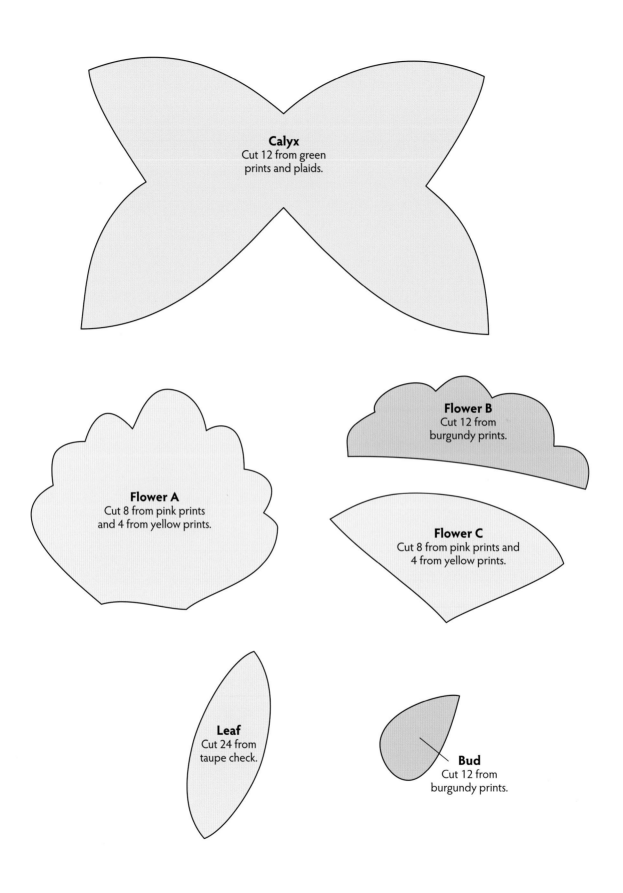

Calyx
Cut 12 from green
prints and plaids.

Flower B
Cut 12 from
burgundy prints.

Flower A
Cut 8 from pink prints
and 4 from yellow prints.

Flower C
Cut 8 from pink prints and
4 from yellow prints.

Leaf
Cut 24 from
taupe check.

Bud
Cut 12 from
burgundy prints.

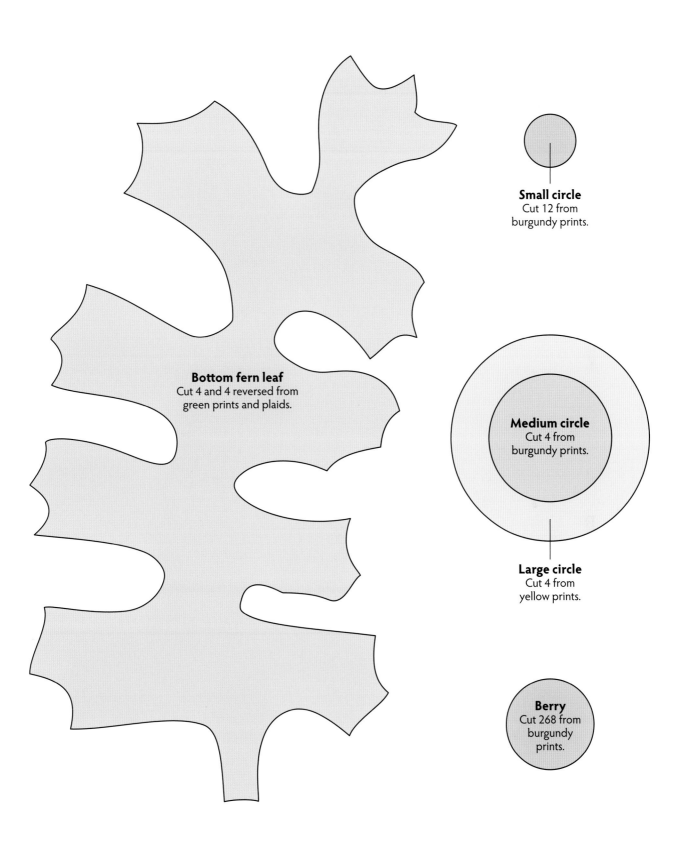

Small circle
Cut 12 from
burgundy prints.

Bottom fern leaf
Cut 4 and 4 reversed from
green prints and plaids.

Medium circle
Cut 4 from
burgundy prints.

Large circle
Cut 4 from
yellow prints.

Berry
Cut 268 from
burgundy
prints.

Gently curving leaves appliquéd in the border add movement to a simply pieced quilt. Soft sage greens and creams create a soothing color palette that would complement any room.

Materials

Yardage is based on 42"-wide fabric.

3⅛ yards of cream print for blocks, sashing, and borders

2¾ yards *total* of assorted green prints for blocks and appliqués

½ yard of green print for binding

3½ yards of fabric for backing

62" × 62" piece of batting

Seam sealant, such as Fray Block

Freezer paper

⅜" bias-tape maker

Water-soluble marker

Cutting

All measurements include ¼" seam allowances.

From the cream print, cut:

- 6 strips, 6½" × 42"; crosscut *1 of the strips* into 4 squares, 6½" × 6½"

- 4 strips, 4¼" × 42"; crosscut into 36 squares, 4¼" × 4¼". Cut the squares into quarters diagonally to yield 144 side triangles.

- 3 strips, 2⅝" × 42"; crosscut into 36 squares, 2⅝" × 2⅝"

- 5 strips, 2½" × 42"; crosscut into 72 squares, 2½" × 2½". Cut the squares in half diagonally to yield 144 corner triangles.

- 15 strips, 1½" × 42"; crosscut *12 of the strips* into:
    7 strips, 1½" × 41½"
    30 strips, 1½" × 6½"

From the assorted green prints, cut a *total* of:

- 144 squares, 2⅝" × 2⅝"

- 6 strips, ⅞" × 42"

From the green print for binding, cut:

- 6 strips, 2¼" × 42"

FINISHED QUILT: 55½" × 55½"
FINISHED BLOCK: 6" × 6"

◆

*Pieced and appliquéd by Dawn Heese;
quilted by Hawthorne Custom Quilts*

Making the Blocks

Press seam allowances in the directions indicated by the arrows.

Lay out four green squares, one cream 2⅝" square, four side triangles, and four corner triangles as shown. Sew all the pieces into diagonal rows. Join the rows to make a block. Make 36 blocks measuring 6½" square, including seam allowances.

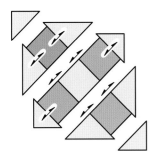

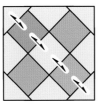

Make 36 blocks,
6½" × 6½".

Appliquéing the Borders

Refer to "Appliqué Techniques" on page 91 for more details. Use the photo on page 24 for placement guidance.

1 Join the cream 6½"-wide strips end to end. From the pieced strip, cut four 43½"-long strips. Seal the edges of each strip using a seam sealant to prevent raveling and distortion during the appliqué process.

2 Join the green ⅞"-wide strips end to end. Using the bias-tape maker and the pieced green strip, prepare four ⅜" × 43½" stems and eight ⅜" × 3½" stems for appliqué. Set aside the shorter stems for the corner blocks.

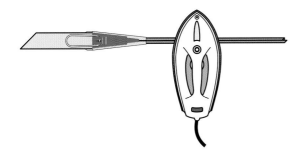

3 Using the border leaf pattern on page 27, trace 84 leaves and 84 reversed leaves onto the dull, nonwaxy side of the freezer paper. Cut out the leaves

on the traced line to make freezer-paper templates. Use your favorite method and the remaining green prints to prepare the leaves for appliqué.

4 Using a water-soluble marker and a long ruler, draw a line along the lengthwise center of a strip from step 1. Pin or baste a 43½"-long stem on the marked line. Position the prepared leaves along the center stem, making sure the leaves are at least ¼" from the outer edges of the strip. Hand appliqué the stem and leaves in place. Make four appliquéd borders.

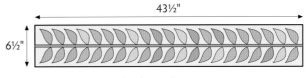

43½"

6½"

Appliqué placement.
Make 4 borders.

Appliquéing the Corner Blocks

1 Using the corner leaf pattern on page 27, trace 16 leaves onto the dull, nonwaxy side of the freezer paper. Cut out the leaves on the traced line to make freezer-paper templates. Use your favorite method and the green prints to prepare the leaves for appliqué.

2 Seal the edges of each cream 6½" square using a seam sealant. Pin two ⅞" × 3½" stems in the center of a cream square to form a right angle, with the strips running into the seam allowance.

3 Position four leaves on a cream square, making sure the leaves are at least ¼" from the outer edges and layering them over the stems with the tips meeting in the center. Appliqué the stems and leaves in place. Make four corner blocks measuring 6½" square, including seam allowances.

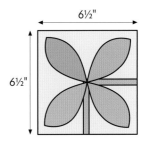

6½"

6½"

Appliqué placement.
Make 4 corner blocks.

Assembling the Quilt Top

1 Join six blocks and five cream 1½" × 6½" strips to make a block row. Make six rows measuring 6½" × 41½", including seam allowances.

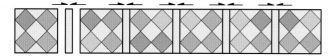

Make 6 block rows,
6½" × 41½".

2 Referring to the quilt assembly diagram below, join the block rows and five cream 1½" × 41½" strips. The quilt top should measure 41½" square, including seam allowances.

3 Sew the remaining two cream 1½" × 41½" strips to the left and right sides of the quilt center. Join the remaining cream 1½"-wide strips end to end. From the pieced strip, cut two 43½"-long strips. Sew these strips to the top and bottom edges.

4 Sew the appliquéd borders to the left and right sides of the quilt, noting the direction of the leaves. Sew an appliquéd corner block to each end of the remaining appliquéd borders, making sure the stems line up. Sew these borders to the top and bottom edges of the quilt, again aligning the stems on the corner blocks and side borders. The quilt top should measure 55½" square.

Quilt assembly

Finishing the Quilt

For more details on any finishing steps, visit
ShopMartingale.com/HowtoQuilt for free
downloadable information.

1 Layer the quilt top with batting and backing;
   baste the layers together.

2 Quilt by hand or machine. The quilt shown is
   machine quilted with curved lines in the blocks
   and outline stitching around the appliqués.

3 Use the green 2¼"-wide strips to make double-
   fold binding. Attach the binding to the quilt.

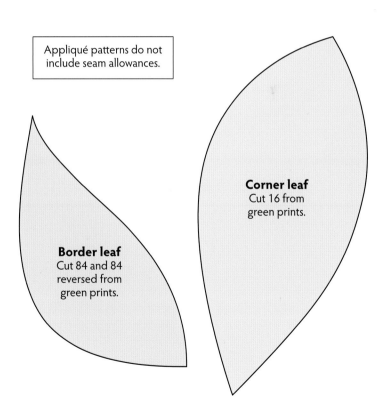

Appliqué patterns do not
include seam allowances.

Corner leaf
Cut 16 from
green prints.

Border leaf
Cut 84 and 84
reversed from
green prints.

The blocks in this quilt started out as Single Wedding Ring blocks, but I changed the color placement, altering the look as my plans progressed. Flying geese make trails above and below the blocks. Perfect for fat quarters, the only areas of the quilt that are not scrappy are the yellow border and the narrow cream border.

◆◼◆

Materials

Yardage is based on 42"-wide fabric. Fat quarters measure 18" × 21".

8 fat quarters *OR* 1⅞ yards *total* of assorted cream prints for blocks

8 fat quarters *OR* 2 yards *total* of assorted navy prints for blocks, cornerstones, outer border, and binding

2 fat quarters *OR* ⅜ yard *total* of assorted yellow prints for blocks

3 fat quarters *OR* ¾ yard *total* of assorted light blue prints for sashing and flying-geese units

⅝ yard of yellow plaid for inner border

¼ yard of cream print for middle border

3⅜ yards of fabric for backing

60" × 66" piece of batting

Cutting

All measurements include ¼" seam allowances.

From the assorted cream prints, cut a *total* of:
- 128 squares, 2⅞" × 2⅞"
- 80 squares, 2½" × 2½"
- 72 squares, 2⅜" × 2⅜"

From the assorted navy prints, cut a *total* of:
- 6 squares, 4¼" × 4¼"
- 128 squares, 2⅞" × 2⅞"
- 12 strips, 2¼" × 21"
- 8 strips, 1½" × 14¾"
- 4 strips, 1½" × 18½"
- 2 strips, 1½" × 17½"
- 9 squares, 1½" × 1½"

From the assorted yellow prints, cut a *total* of:
- 64 squares, 2½" × 2½"

(Continued on page 31)

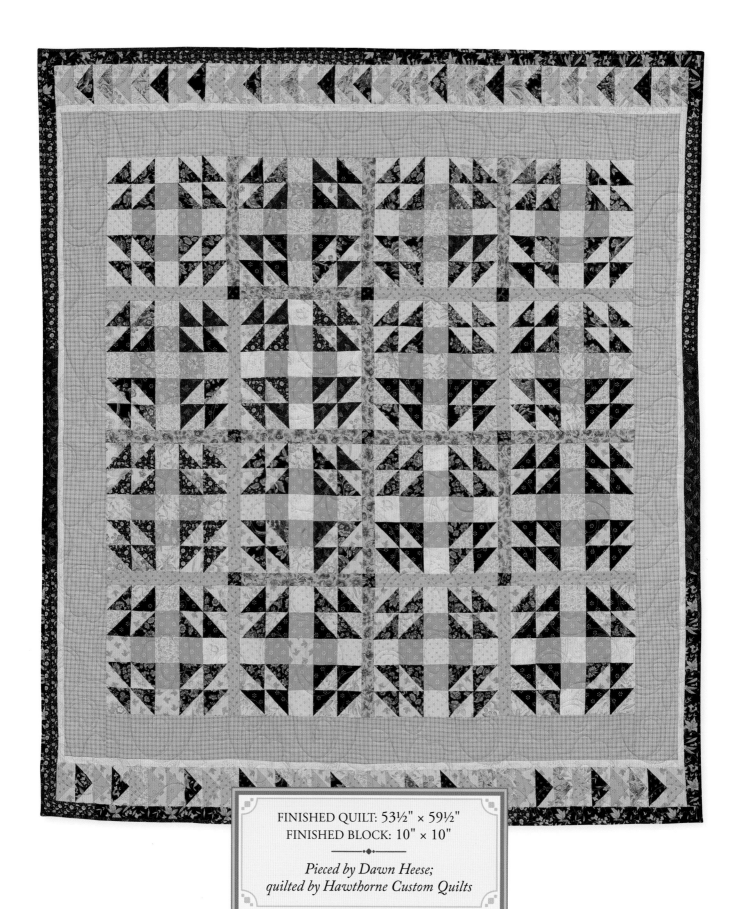

FINISHED QUILT: 53½" × 59½"
FINISHED BLOCK: 10" × 10"

Pieced by Dawn Heese;
quilted by Hawthorne Custom Quilts

(Continued from page 29)

From the assorted light blue prints, cut a *total* of:
- 24 strips, 1½" × 10½"
- 12 squares, 4¼" × 4¼"

From the yellow plaid, cut:
- 5 strips, 4" × 42"

From the cream print for middle border, cut:
- 6 strips, 1" × 42"

Making the Blocks

Press seam allowances in the directions indicated by the arrows.

1 Draw a diagonal line from corner to corner on the wrong side of the cream 2⅞" squares. Layer a marked square on a navy 2⅞" square, right sides together. Sew ¼" from both sides of the drawn line. Cut the unit apart on the marked line to make two half-square-triangle units. Make 256 units measuring 2½" square, including seam allowances.

Make 256 units,
2½" × 2½".

2 Lay out 16 half-square-triangle units, four yellow 2½" squares, and five cream 2½" squares in five rows. Sew all the pieces into rows and then join the rows. Make 16 blocks measuring 10½" square, including seam allowances.

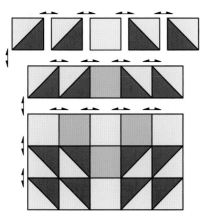

Make 16 blocks,
10½" × 10½".

TRIANGLE PAPERS TO THE RESCUE

Whenever I need to make a lot of matching half-square-triangle units, I use triangle papers such as Triangles on a Roll or Triangulations software. Either of these products allows me to make a bunch of triangle units quickly and accurately. If you want to use triangle papers, do not cut the cream and navy 2⅞" squares. Instead, skip step 1 of "Making the Blocks" and follow the directions on the package to cut the pieces and make the half-square-triangle units.

Making the Flying-Geese Border

1 Draw a diagonal line from corner to corner on the wrong side of the cream 2⅜" squares. Align two squares on opposite corners of a navy or light blue 4¼" square, right sides together. The marked squares should overlap in the center. Sew ¼" from both sides of the drawn line. Cut the unit apart on the drawn line to make two units.

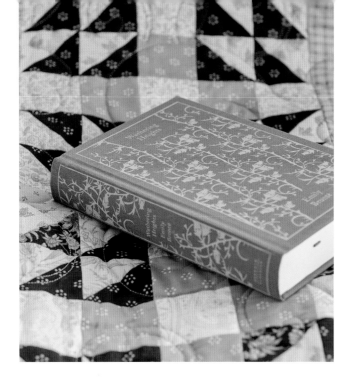

Assembling the Quilt Top

1. Join four blocks and three light blue strips to make a block row. Make four rows measuring 10½" × 43½", including seam allowances.

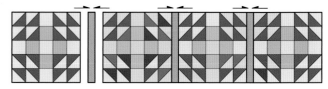

Make 4 block rows,
10½" × 43½".

2. Join four light blue strips with three navy 1½" squares to make a sashing row. Make three rows measuring 1½" × 43½", including seam allowances.

Make 3 sashing rows,
1½" × 43½".

3. Referring to the quilt assembly diagram on page 33, join the block rows and sashing rows. The quilt center should measure 43½" square, including seam allowances.

4. Join the yellow plaid 4"-wide strips end to end. From the pieced strip, cut two 50½"-long strips and two 43½"-long strips. Sew the shorter strips to the top and bottom edges of the quilt center. Sew the longer strips to the left and right sides. The quilt top should measure 50½" square, including seam allowances.

5. Join the cream 1"-wide strips end to end. From the pieced strip, cut two 51½"-long strips and two 50½"-long strips. Sew the shorter strips to the top and bottom edges of the quilt center. Sew the longer strips to the left and right sides. The quilt top should measure 51½" square, including seam allowances.

6. Sew the flying-geese borders to the top and bottom of the quilt, noting the direction of the flying geese. The quilt top should measure 51½" × 57½", including seam allowances.

2. Place a marked square on the corner of a navy or light blue triangle from step 1, right sides together, noting the direction of the marked line. Sew ¼" from both sides of the drawn line. Cut the unit apart on the drawn line. Repeat with another marked square and the remaining unit from step 1 to yield four flying-geese units. The units should measure 2" × 3½", including seam allowances. Make 24 navy and 48 light blue units. Two navy and two light blue units are extra.

Make 24 units,
2" × 3½". Make 48 units,
2" × 3½".

3. Join 23 light blue and 11 navy flying-geese units in random order to make a border. Make two borders measuring 3½" × 51½", including seam allowances.

Make 2 borders,
3½" × 51½".

7 Join four navy 1½" × 14¾" strips end to end to make a side border measuring 1½" × 57½", including seam allowances. Make two and sew them to the left and right sides of the quilt. The quilt top should measure 53½" × 57½", including seam allowances.

8 Join one navy 1½" × 17½" strip and two navy 1½" × 18½" strips to make the top border measuring 1½" × 53½". Repeat to make the bottom border. Sew the borders to the top and bottom edges. The quilt top should measure 53½" × 59½".

Finishing the Quilt

For more details on any finishing steps, visit ShopMartingale.com/HowtoQuilt for free downloadable information.

1 Layer the quilt top with batting and backing; baste the layers together.

2 Quilt by hand or machine. The quilt shown is machine quilted with an allover swirl and leaf design.

3 Use the navy 2¼"-wide strips to make a scrappy double-fold binding. Attach the binding to the quilt.

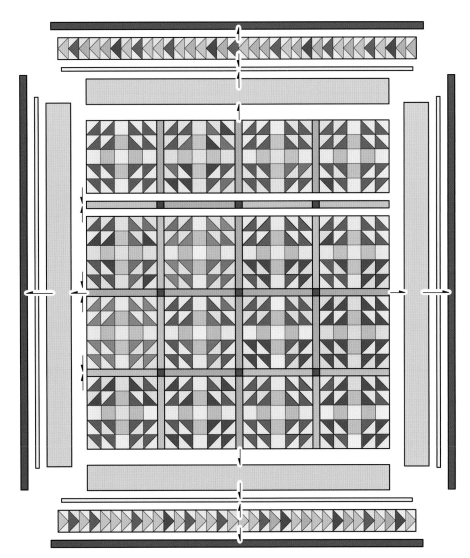

Quilt assembly

MERRYAN

The gentle curves of vintage-inspired Pineapple blocks in this quilt are complemented by the geometric pieced borders. A simple palette creates a soft but graphic quilt.

Materials

Yardage is based on 42"-wide fabric.

1⅜ yards of cream woven for blocks and middle border

2⅛ yards of green check for appliqué, pieced border, and outer border

1⅛ yard of red print for appliqué, pieced border, and binding

½ yard of red stripe for appliqué and pieced border

3¼ yards of fabric for backing

57" × 57" piece of batting

Seam sealant, such as Fray Block

Freezer paper

WOVEN CHECKS AND STRIPES

I love the added texture that using yarn-dyed fabrics brings to my finished quilts. Rather than printing a motif, checks, or stripes onto fabric blanks, the fibers are dyed first, then woven to create the designs. This means the front and back of the fabric look the same, as the colors are woven together rather than printed on top. If you're looking for something similar, ask your local quilt shop or search online for Diamond Textiles, the producer of the fabrics I used.

Cutting

All measurements include ¼" seam allowances.

From the cream woven, cut:
- 2 strips, 18½" × 42"; crosscut into 4 squares, 18½" × 18½"
- 5 strips, 1½" × 42"

From the green check, cut:
- 3 strips, 4¼" × 42"; crosscut into 24 squares, 4¼" × 4¼". Cut the squares into quarters diagonally to yield 96 side triangles.
- 5 strips, 3½" × 42"
- 1 strip, 2⅜" × 42"; crosscut into 8 squares, 2⅜" × 2⅜". Cut the squares in half diagonally to yield 16 corner triangles.

From the red print, cut:
- 2 strips, 2⅝" × 42"; crosscut into 28 squares, 2⅝" × 2⅝"
- 6 strips, 2¼" × 42"

From the red stripe, cut:
- 2 strips, 2⅝" × 42"; crosscut into 24 squares, 2⅝" × 2⅝"

FINISHED QUILT: 50½" × 50½"
FINISHED BLOCK: 18" × 18"

Appliquéd and pieced by Dawn Heese;
quilted by Hawthorne Custom Quilts

Appliquéing the Blocks

Refer to "Appliqué Techniques" on page 91 as needed for more details.

1 Seal the edges of each cream square using a seam sealant to prevent raveling and distortion during the appliqué process.

2 Using the patterns on pages 40 and 41, trace the shapes the indicated number of times onto the dull, nonwaxy side of the freezer paper. Cut out the shapes on the traced line to make freezer-paper templates. Cut the number of pieces noted on the patterns from the fabrics indicated. Use your favorite method to prepare the shapes for appliqué.

3 Fold a cream square in half vertically and then horizontally; finger-press to establish centering creases. Unfold and then fold the square diagonally in both directions; finger-press. Using the creases as a guide, place a pineapple leaf on a cream square. Position the green scalloped arcs around the pineapple leaf, tucking the ends under the edges. Layer the red arcs on top of the green ones, tucking the ends under the pineapple leaf. Add the remaining shapes. Use your favorite method to appliqué the shapes in place. Repeat to make four blocks measuring 18½" square, including seam allowances. Set aside the remaining prepared red circle until after the blocks have been joined.

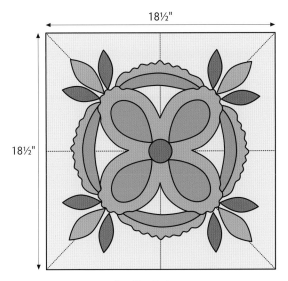

Appliqué placement

Assembling the Quilt Top

Refer to the quilt assembly diagram on page 39 as needed throughout. Press seam allowances in the directions indicated by the arrows.

1 Lay out the blocks in two rows of two blocks each. Sew the blocks into rows and then join the rows. Appliqué the remaining red circle on top of the intersection of the four seams, as shown in the photo on page 36.

2 Lay out five red print squares, seven red stripe squares, 22 green side triangles, and four green corner triangles as shown. Sew the pieces into diagonal rows and then join the rows to make the top border. In the same way, join six red print squares, six red stripe squares, 22 green side triangles, and four green corner triangles to make the bottom border. The borders should each measure 3½" × 36½", including seam allowances. Sew the borders to the top and bottom edges of the quilt center.

Make 1 top border,
3½" × 36½".

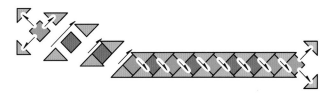

Make 1 bottom border,
3½" × 36½".

3 Lay out eight red print squares, six red stripe squares, 26 green side triangles, and four green corner triangles as shown. Sew the pieces into diagonal rows and then join the rows to make the left side

border. In the same way, join nine red print squares, five red stripe squares, 26 green side triangles, and four green corner triangles to make the right side border. The borders should measure 3½" × 42½", including seam allowances. Sew the borders to the left and right sides of the quilt. The quilt top should measure 42½" square, including seam allowances.

Make 1 left side border,
3½" × 42½".

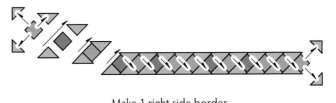

Make 1 right side border,
3½" × 42½".

EASIER THAN IT LOOKS!

Don't be intimidated by the pieced borders on this quilt. The triangles will be taller than your squares. Just remember to always align the flat edge of the triangle with the edge of the square you're sewing it to. The extra tip of the triangles will be taken up in the seam allowances when you join the units. The result will be a great patchwork counterpoint to the curvy appliqué blocks.

4 Join the cream 1½"-wide strips end to end. From the pieced strip, cut 44½"-long strips and two 42½"-long strips. Sew the shorter strips to the top and bottom of the quilt. Sew the longer strips to the left and right sides. The quilt top should measure 44½" square, including seam allowances.

5 Join the green 3½"-wide strips end to end. From the pieced strip, cut two 50½"-long strips and two 44½"-long strips. Sew the shorter strips to the top and bottom of the quilt. Sew the longer strips to the left and right sides. The quilt top should measure 50½" square.

Finishing the Quilt

For more details on any finishing steps, visit ShopMartingale.com/HowtoQuilt for free downloadable information.

1 Layer the quilt top with batting and backing; baste the layers together.

2 Quilt by hand or machine. The quilt shown is machine quilted with echo stitching around the appliqués. A feather motif is stitched in the background and outer border. Curved lines are stitched in the pieced border.

3 Use the red print 2¼"-wide strips to make double-fold binding. Attach the binding to the quilt.

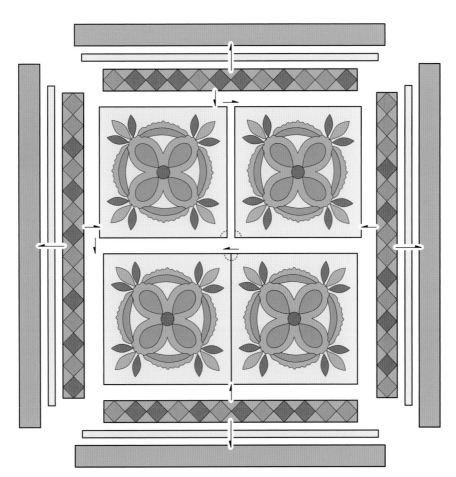

Quilt assembly

Merryan

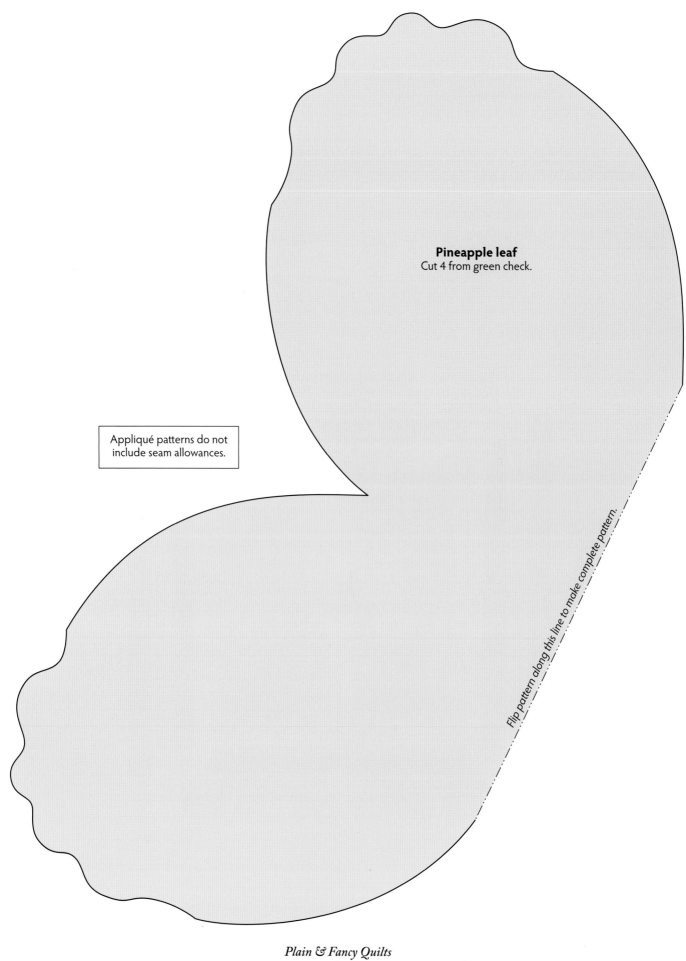

Pineapple leaf
Cut 4 from green check.

Appliqué patterns do not
include seam allowances.

Flip pattern along this line to make complete pattern.

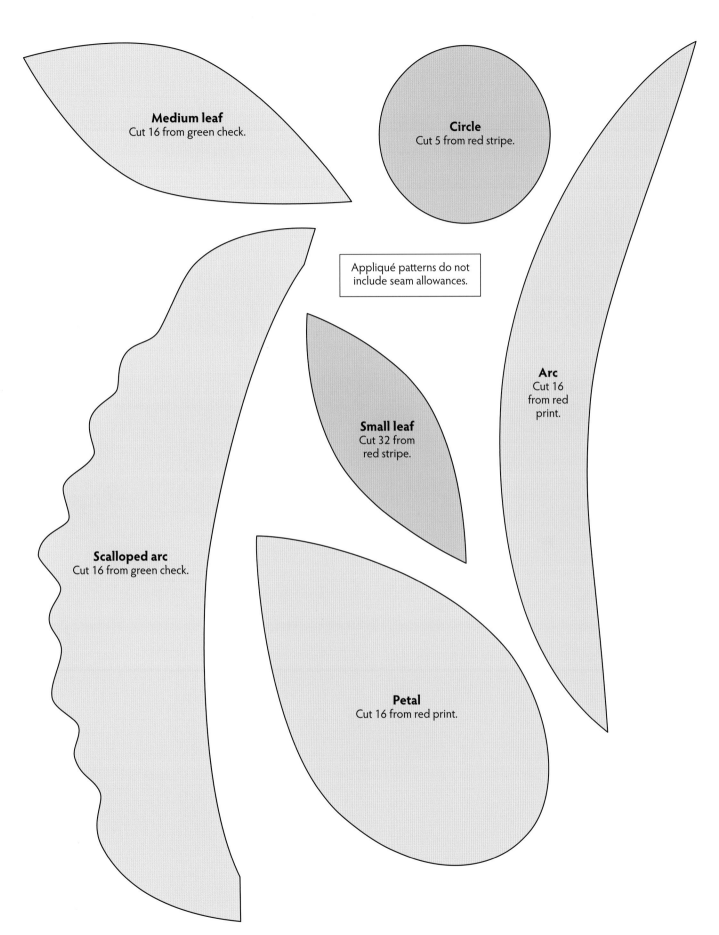

Medium leaf
Cut 16 from green check.

Circle
Cut 5 from red stripe.

Appliqué patterns do not
include seam allowances.

Arc
Cut 16
from red
print.

Small leaf
Cut 32 from
red stripe.

Scalloped arc
Cut 16 from green check.

Petal
Cut 16 from red print.

Merryan

HARLEQUIN

Delicate leaves curl around folk-art tulips on this beautiful wool table mat. A red wool scalloped border finishes the piece with a flourish.

Materials

Wool yardage is based on 54"-wide fabric.

⅞ yard of oatmeal wool for background of appliqué and backing

15" × 24" piece of red plaid wool for scalloped borders and berries

12" × 18" piece of green wool for stems and leaves

6" × 15" piece of light red stripe wool for tulips and tulip points

6" × 15" piece of pink plaid wool for tulips and tulip points

4" × 10" piece of gold wool for berries and center circle

Pink, green, red, and gold 6-strand embroidery floss

Cream pearl cotton, size 8

Freezer paper

Pencil or white chalk marker

Long-neck stapler

Safety pins

Cutting

All measurements include ¼" seam allowances.

From the oatmeal wool, cut:
- 1 square, 28" × 28"
- 1 square, 22" × 22"

From the green wool, cut:
- 4 strips, ¼" × 11"
- 4 strips, ¼" × 6"
- 4 strips, ¼" × 5"
- 4 strips, ¼" × 2½"

From the red plaid wool, cut:
- 4 strips, 3" × 24"; set aside for scallops

FINISHED TABLE MAT: 26" × 26"
FINISHED BLOCK: 22" × 22"

Appliquéd by Dawn Heese

Appliquéing the Table Mat

Refer to "Embroidery Stitches" on page 95 as needed.

1 Referring to "Wool Appliqué" on page 93, trace the tulip, leaves, berries, and center circle patterns on page 47 the indicated number of times onto the dull, nonwaxy side of the freezer paper. Cut out the shapes directly on the line. Use the freezer-paper templates to cut the number of pieces noted on the patterns from the fabrics indicated. **Note:** when cutting the dark red berries, cut them from the wool that's left over after cutting the strips to be used for the scallops.

2 Using the appliqué placement diagram below as a guide, place the shapes on the oatmeal 22" square, starting with the center circle. I generally eyeball the placement for folk-art pieces like this, but if you want guidelines, you can use a 24" quilting ruler laid on top as a diagonal guide for placing the stems. Or, you can fold the fabric in half and hand baste temporary guidelines. Place the green 11"-long strips on the diagonal lines and curve them as shown, tucking the ends under the center circle. Place each green 5"-long strip to the left of the center stem, tucking the end under the center stem just a bit. Add the green 6"-long strips, tucking the end under the center stem. Staple the shapes in place.

3 Place the tulips in the center and add the tulip petals. Place a green 2½"-long strip at the bottom of each tulip, tucking the ends under the tulip and center circle. Add the leaves and berries and staple all the pieces to the background.

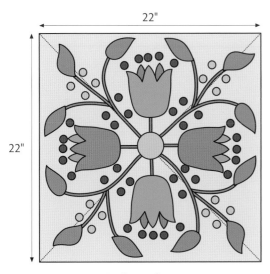

22"

22"

Appliqué placement

4 Using two strands of green floss, cross-stitch over the stems and fly stitch the center of each leaf. Use six strands of floss and a stem stitch to stitch a stem for each berry. Using two strands of red or gold floss and a straight stitch, secure each berry with a spoke pattern. In the middle of the center circle, use three strands of gold floss to make a French knot. Use two strands of gold floss to stem-stitch a circle and then make oversized buttonhole stitches from the circle to the outer edge. Using three strands of pink floss, make a large chevron stitch across each tulip. Using two strands of coordinating floss, whipstitch around the tulips and leaves. Remove all staples.

Finishing the Mat

1 Trace the scallop pattern on pattern sheet 1 onto the dull, nonwaxy side of the freezer paper. Cut out the shape directly on the line. Use the freezer-paper template to cut four scalloped borders from the red plaid wool 3"-wide strips.

2 To attach the scalloped borders, tuck ½" of the straight edge of the scalloped border under the appliquéd block. Pin it in place on each side. Using the pearl cotton, blanket-stitch around the perimeter of the block, making sure to stitch through all the layers.

3 Layer the finished mat right side up on the oatmeal 28" square. Safety-pin the two layers together securely and then cut away the excess backing to match the scalloped edges. While still pinned, stitch the layers together using three strands of red floss and a running stitch, approximately ¼" from the outer edge.

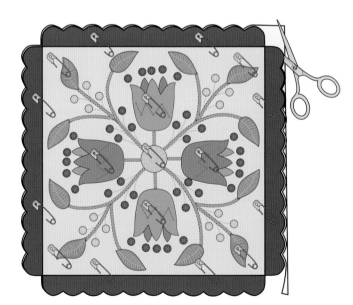

Trim backing.

4 Remove the pins, staples, and any pencil markings. Lightly press with steam.

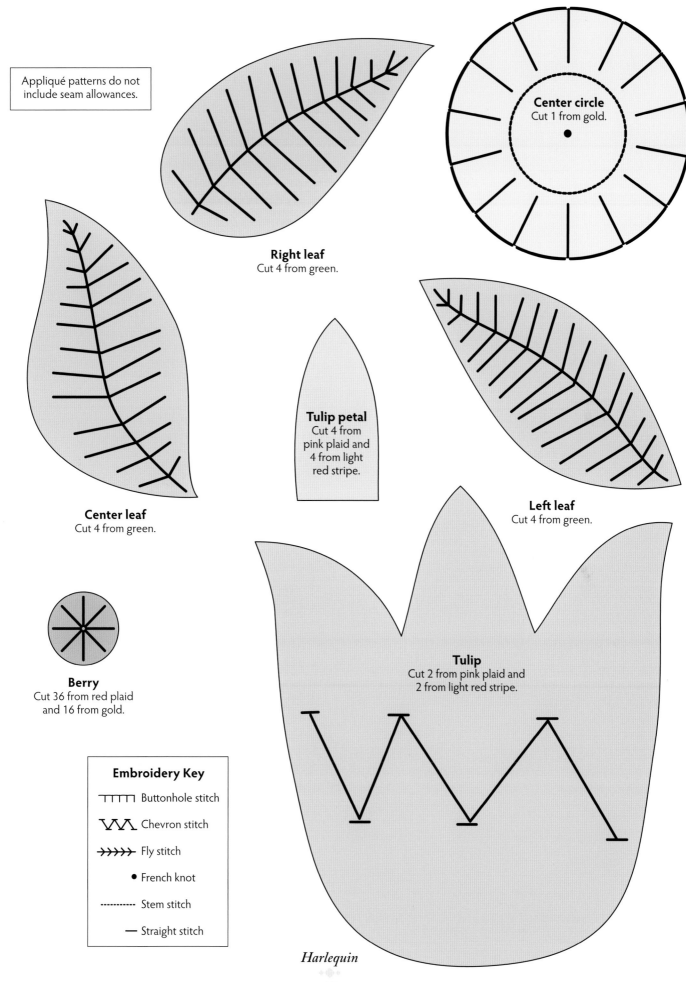

Appliqué patterns do not include seam allowances.

Center circle
Cut 1 from gold.

Right leaf
Cut 4 from green.

Center leaf
Cut 4 from green.

Tulip petal
Cut 4 from pink plaid and 4 from light red stripe.

Left leaf
Cut 4 from green.

Berry
Cut 36 from red plaid and 16 from gold.

Tulip
Cut 2 from pink plaid and 2 from light red stripe.

Embroidery Key

⊤⊤⊤⊤⊤	Buttonhole stitch
∨∨∨	Chevron stitch
⟩⟩⟩⟩⟩	Fly stitch
•	French knot
---------	Stem stitch
—	Straight stitch

Harlequin

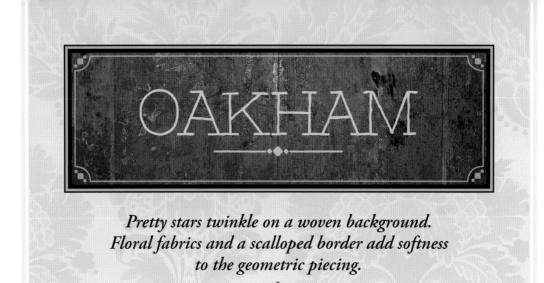

*Pretty stars twinkle on a woven background.
Floral fabrics and a scalloped border add softness
to the geometric piecing.*

◆◈◆

Materials

*Yardage is based on 42"-wide fabric. Fat eighths
measure 9" × 21".*

2¼ yards of cream woven stripe for blocks and sashing
(see "Woven Checks and Stripes" on page 34 for
more information)

7 fat eighths *OR* ¾ yard *total* of assorted prints
for blocks

1½ yards of green floral for blocks, border, and binding

⅛ yard of green paisley for blocks

5" × 16" piece of red print for blocks

3½ yards of fabric for backing

61" × 61" piece of batting

Freezer paper

Water-soluble marker

Cutting

All measurements include ¼" seam allowances.

From the cream stripe, cut:
- 6 strips, 6½" × 42"; crosscut into 12 strips,
  6½" × 15½"
- 5 strips, 3¼" × 42"; crosscut into 50 squares,
  3¼" × 3¼". Cut the squares into quarters diagonally
  to yield 200 triangles.
- 7 strips, 2½" × 42"; crosscut into 100 squares,
  2½" × 2½"

From the assorted prints, cut a *total* of:
- 25 pairs of 2 matching squares, 3¼" × 3¼"; cut the
  squares into quarters diagonally to yield 25 sets of
  8 matching triangles (200 total)
- 25 squares, 2½" × 2½"

From the green floral, cut:
- 8 strips, 3½" × 42"; crosscut *2 of the strips* into
  11 pieces, 3½" × 6½"

From the remainder of the green floral, cut *on the bias*:
- 2¼"-wide strips to total 235"

From the green paisley, cut:
- 1 strip, 3½" × 42"; crosscut into 5 strips, 3½" × 6½"

From the red print, cut:
- 4 squares, 3½" × 3½"

FINISHED QUILT: 54½" × 54½"
FINISHED BLOCK: 15" × 15"

Pieced and quilted by Dawn Heese

Making the Blocks

Press seam allowances in the directions indicated by the arrows.

1 Lay out two cream and two matching print triangles. Sew the triangles into pairs and then join the pairs to make an hourglass unit. Make 25 sets of four matching units measuring 2½" square, including seam allowances.

Make 25 sets of 4 matching units,
2½" × 2½".

2 Lay out four cream 2½" squares, four matching hourglass units, and one print 2½" square in three rows as shown. Sew the pieces into rows and then join the rows to make a star unit. Make 25 units measuring 6½" square, including seam allowances.

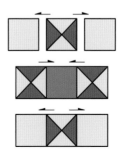 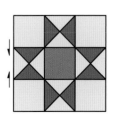

Make 25 units,
6½" × 6½".

Oakham

3 Lay out four star units, four green floral or paisley 3½" × 6½" pieces, and one red square in three rows. Sew the pieces into rows and then join the rows to make a block. Make four blocks measuring 15½" square, including seam allowances. Set aside the remaining star units for the sashing rows.

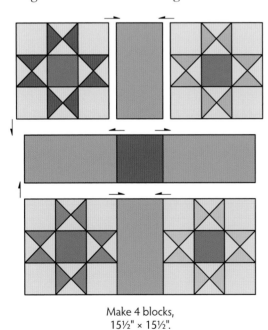

Make 4 blocks,
15½" × 15½".

Assembling the Quilt Top

1 Join three star units and two cream 6½" × 15½" strips to make a sashing row. Make three rows measuring 6½" × 48½", including seam allowances.

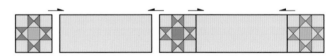

Make 3 sashing rows,
6½" × 48½".

2 Join two blocks and three cream 6½" × 15½" strips to make a block row. Make two rows measuring 15½" × 48½", including seam allowances.

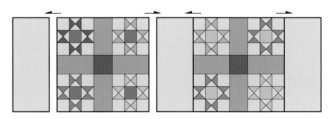

Make 2 block rows,
15½" × 48½".

3 Referring to the quilt assembly diagram on page 53, join the sashing rows and block rows. The quilt center should measure 48½" square, including seam allowances.

4 Join the green 3½"-wide strips end to end. From the pieced strip, cut two 54½"-long strips and two 48½"-long strips. Sew the shorter strips to the left and right sides of the quilt center. Sew the longer strips to the top and bottom edges. The quilt top should measure 54½" square.

Finishing the Quilt

For more details on any finishing steps, visit ShopMartingale.com/HowtoQuilt for free downloadable information.

1 Layer the quilt top with batting and backing; baste the layers together.

2 Quilt by hand or machine. The quilt shown is machine quilted with vertical and horizontal lines to form a grid.

3 Trace the corner and side scallop patterns on pattern sheet 1 onto the dull, nonwaxy side of the freezer paper. Cut out the shapes on the marked line.

4 To mark the scallops on the outer border, align the straight edge of each template with the seamline. Using a water-soluble marker, trace the corner scallop in all four corners. Then trace side scallops A and B on each side of the quilt. The quilt may have shrunk after quilting, so the side scallops may not fit exactly. As you trace, adjust the length of the side scallops to fit. Do *not* cut the scallops yet.

5 Use the green 2¼"-wide bias strips to make double-fold binding. Aligning the raw edges of the binding with the drawn scallops, sew the binding to the quilt. Start on the roundest part of a scallop and use a ¼" seam allowance. Stitch to the valley of the scallop. Stop with the needle down, pivot, and sew back out of the valley, taking care to avoid pleats.

6 Once the binding has been attached to the quilt, trim the excess border and batting even with the edge of the binding. Turn the binding to the back of the quilt and stitch in place, easing as needed to fit the peaks and valleys of the curves.

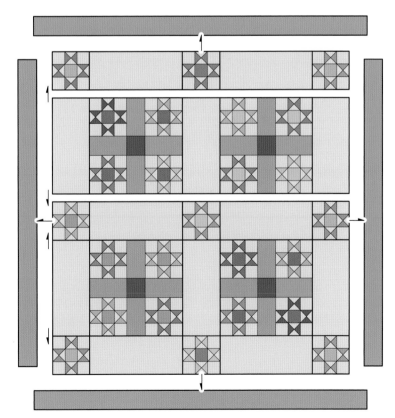

Quilt assembly

Oakham

This pretty wool mat was inspired by an antique hooked rug. The fern leaves frame the pot of folksy flowers and wavy scallops create a fun finish.

◆●◆

Materials

Cotton yardage is based on 42"-wide fabric.

16" × 26" piece of brown/black plaid wool for background

16" × 20" piece of light blue wool for bow, pot, and scallops

9" × 17" piece of dark green wool for leaves and stems

5" × 11" piece of light green wool for leaves and stems

5" × 6" piece of yellow wool for flowers and pot

4" × 5" piece of red wool for flowers

5" × 6" piece of khaki wool for pot and bow center

⅝ yard of black solid cotton for backing

½ yard of fusible web, such as HeatnBond Lite

Freezer paper

Green, blue, red, yellow, khaki, and black 3-strand Valdani embroidery floss

Gray pearl cotton, size 8

Long-neck stapler

Cutting

All measurements include ¼" seam allowances.

From the dark green wool, cut:
- 2 strips, ¼" × 15"
- 2 strips, ¼" × 4½"

From the light green wool, cut:
- 2 strips, ¼" × 8"
- 1 strip, ¼" × 3½"

From the black solid cotton, cut:
- 1 piece, 18" × 29"

Appliquéing the Table Mat

Refer to "Embroidery Stitches" on page 95 as needed. Use two strands of embroidery floss unless otherwise specified.

1 Referring to "Wool Appliqué" on page 93, trace the background on pattern sheet 2 and the pot, flower, leaves, and circle patterns on pages 58 and 59 the indicated number of times onto the dull, nonwaxy side of the freezer paper. Cut out the shapes directly on the line. Use the freezer-paper templates to cut the number of pieces noted on the patterns from the fabrics indicated.

2. Using the placement diagram as a guide, position the shapes on the background, beginning with the two dark green 15"-long strips, placing the strips about 3½" from the upper curved edge. Place the light and dark green fern leaves on each side of the stems. Place the ribbon bows and tails in the center of the stems. Staple them in place. Place a khaki circle in the center of the bow and staple in place.

3. Place the pot on the background, about ½" from the bottom edge; staple it in place. Add the pot rim and foot. Add the blue circles to the pot. Position the light green 8"-long stems and curve them downward. Place the light green 3½"-long stem in the center of the pot. Add the dark green 4½"-long stems on each side of the center stem. Tuck one end of each stem underneath the pot rim. Position the flower, flower centers, and leaf shapes on the background. Staple all the shapes in place.

4. Use green floss and a couch stitch to secure the stems. Whipstitch around all the shapes using matching thread. Remove all staples.

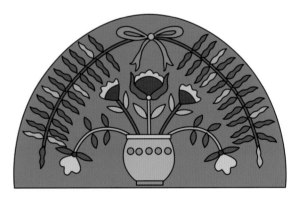

Appliqué placement

Finishing the Mat

1. Trace the scallop patterns on pattern sheet 2 onto the dull, nonwaxy side of the freezer paper. Cut out the shapes directly on the line. Use the freezer-paper templates to cut the two pieces of the scalloped border from the blue wool.

FINISHED TABLE MAT: 28" × 17"

———◆———

Appliquéd by Dawn Heese

2 To attach the scallops, tuck the smooth edge ½" under the appliquéd piece, slightly overlapping the scallop shapes where the two pieces meet. Pin in place. Using blue floss, blanket-stitch the two scallop pieces together. Using black floss, blanket-stitch along the overlapped edge.

3 Fuse the fusible web to the wrong side of the black cotton piece, following the manufacturer's instructions. Center the appliquéd mat on the black piece, wrong sides together. Fuse in place and cut away the excess backing to match the scalloped edges. Using the blue pearl cotton, blanket-stitch around the perimeter of the mat, making sure to stitch through all the layers. Blanket-stitch along the bottom edges using black floss.

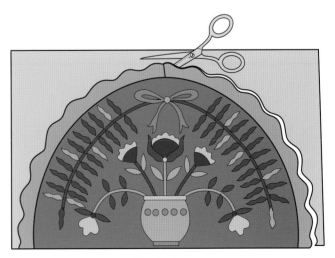

Trim backing.

Fernhill

57

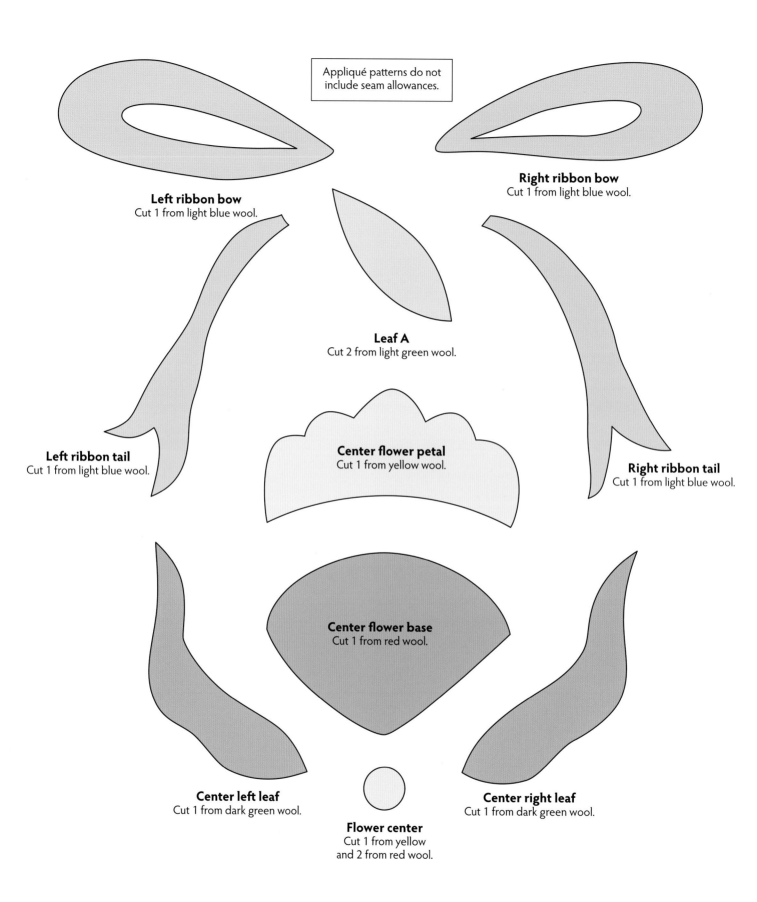

Appliqué patterns do not include seam allowances.

Left ribbon bow
Cut 1 from light blue wool.

Right ribbon bow
Cut 1 from light blue wool.

Leaf A
Cut 2 from light green wool.

Left ribbon tail
Cut 1 from light blue wool.

Center flower petal
Cut 1 from yellow wool.

Right ribbon tail
Cut 1 from light blue wool.

Center flower base
Cut 1 from red wool.

Center left leaf
Cut 1 from dark green wool.

Center right leaf
Cut 1 from dark green wool.

Flower center
Cut 1 from yellow
and 2 from red wool.

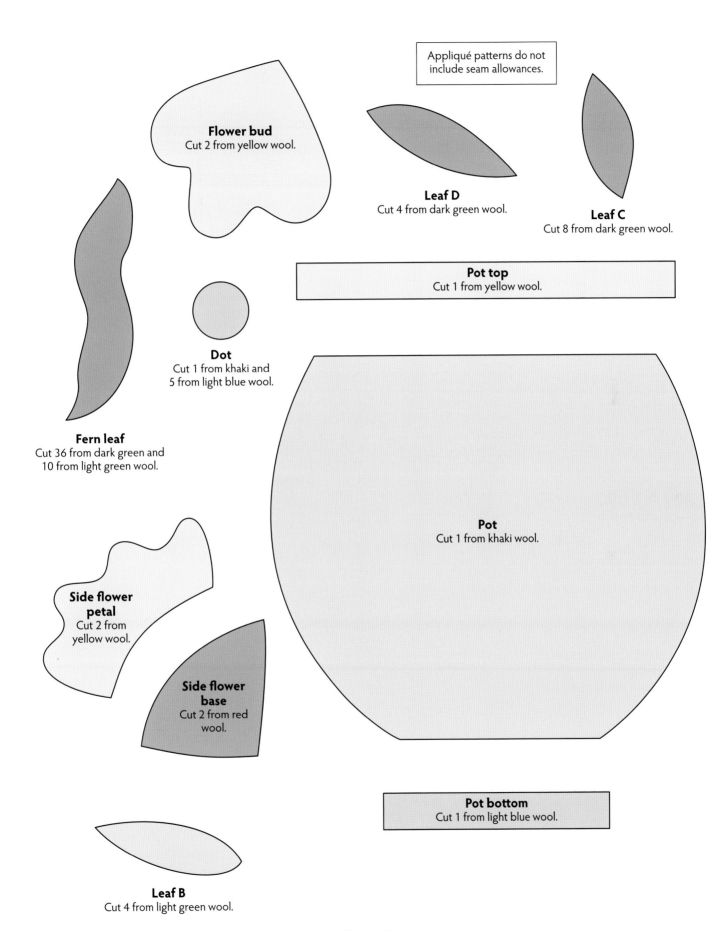

Flower bud
Cut 2 from yellow wool.

Leaf D
Cut 4 from dark green wool.

Leaf C
Cut 8 from dark green wool.

Appliqué patterns do not
include seam allowances.

Pot top
Cut 1 from yellow wool.

Dot
Cut 1 from khaki and
5 from light blue wool.

Fern leaf
Cut 36 from dark green and
10 from light green wool.

Pot
Cut 1 from khaki wool.

**Side flower
petal**
Cut 2 from
yellow wool.

**Side flower
base**
Cut 2 from red
wool.

Pot bottom
Cut 1 from light blue wool.

Leaf B
Cut 4 from light green wool.

Fernhill

It may be small, but this quilt is loaded with charm. Scrappy backgrounds soften the geometric blocks, making them blend together, while gentle vines wind around the border. Did you notice the subtle variations in the four border fabrics?

◆◆◆

Materials

Yardage is based on 42"-wide fabric.

2½ yards *total* of assorted cream woven plaids and stripes for blocks and outer border. (Note that you'll need at least ¼ yard each of 4 of the fabrics to use for the borders.)

¾ yard of black woven plaid for blocks, inner border, and binding

½ yard of green woven stripe for blocks, vines, leaves, and corner flowers

1½ yards *total* of assorted blue, rust, and pink woven plaids and stripes for blocks and leaves

2½ yards of fabric for backing

44" × 50" piece of batting

Seam sealant, such as Fray Block

Freezer paper

¼" bias-tape maker

Cutting

All measurements include ¼" seam allowances.

From the assorted cream plaids and stripes, cut:
- 4 strips, 6½" × 42"; crosscut into:
    2 strips, 6½" × 37½"
    2 strips, 6½" × 31½"
- 20 sets of 2 matching squares, 2⅞" × 2⅞" (40 total)
- 20 sets of 4 matching pieces, 1½" × 2½" (80 total)

From the black plaid, cut:
- 5 strips, 2¼" × 42"
- 4 strips, 1" × 42"; crosscut into:
    2 strips, 1" × 30½"
    2 strips, 1" × 25½"

From the green stripe, cut *on the bias:*
- ½"-wide strips to total 144"

From the black, green, and assorted plaids and stripes, cut 20 matching sets of:
- 2 squares, 2⅞" × 2⅞" (40 total)
- 4 pieces, 1½" × 2½" (80 total)
- 1 square, 2½" × 2½" (20 total)

FINISHED QUILT: 37½" × 43½"
FINISHED BLOCK: 6" × 6"

◆

*Pieced, appliquéd, and quilted
by Dawn Heese*

Plain & Fancy Quilts

Making the Blocks

1 Draw a diagonal line from corner to corner on the wrong side of the cream 2⅞" squares. Layer a marked square on one of the assorted plaid and striped 2⅞" squares, right sides together. Sew ¼" from both sides of the drawn line. Cut the unit apart on the marked line to make two half-square-triangle units that measure 2½" square, including seam allowances. Make 20 sets of four matching units (80 total).

Make 20 sets of 4 matching units, 2½" × 2½".

2 Using the same cream and plaid or stripe fabrics as in step 1, join a cream and a plaid 1½" × 2½" piece to make a side unit measuring 2½" square, including seam allowances. Make 20 sets of four matching units (80 total).

Make 20 sets of 4 matching units, 2½" × 2½".

3 Referring to the diagram, lay out a matched set of four half-square-triangle units, four side units, and one matching 2½" square in three rows. Sew all the pieces into rows and then join the rows. Make 20 blocks measuring 6½" square, including seam allowances.

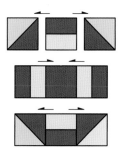 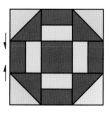

Make 20 blocks, 6½" × 6½".

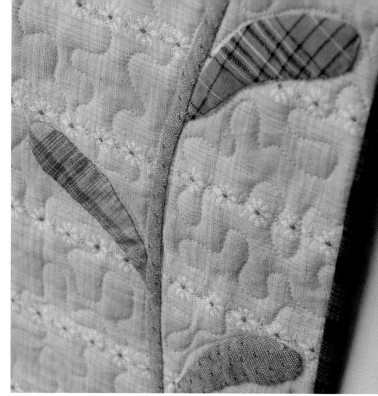

As you're making the blocks, you can use one color of woven fabric for each block as instructed, or you can mix the creams and colors as I did in many blocks in the quilt pictured on page 62.

MIX IT UP

As you're making the blocks, you can use one color of woven fabric for each block as instructed, or you can mix the creams and colors as I did in many blocks in the quilt pictured on page 62.

Assembling the Quilt Top

1 Referring to the quilt assembly diagram below, lay out the blocks in five rows of four blocks each. Sew the blocks into rows and then join the rows. The quilt center should measure 24½" × 30½", including seam allowances.

2 Sew the black 1" × 30½" strips to the left and right sides of the quilt. Sew the black 1" × 25½" strips to the top and bottom edges. The quilt top should measure 25½" × 31½", including seam allowances.

3 Sew the cream 6½" × 31½" strips to the left and right sides of the quilt top. Sew the cream 6½" × 37½" strips to the top and bottom edges. The quilt top should measure 37½" × 43½".

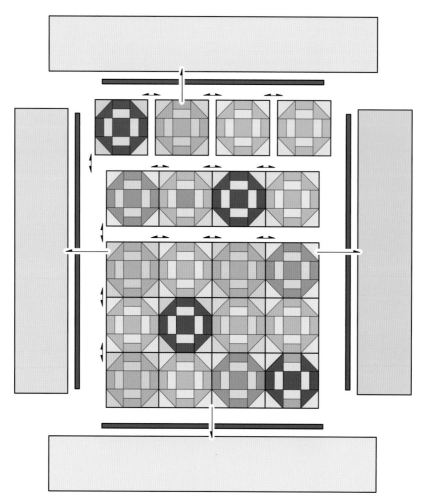

Quilt assembly

Appliquéing the Border

Refer to "Appliqué Techniques" on page 91 as needed for more details. Use the photo on page 62 for placement guidance.

1 Seal the edges of the outer border using a seam sealant to prevent raveling and distortion.

2 Join the green ½"-wide strips end to end. Use the bias-tape maker and the green strip to make the vine. Lay the vine on the outer border in a casual wave around the quilt center. Pin in place.

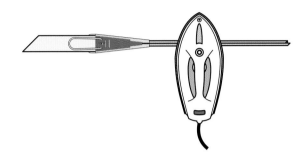

3 Using the leaf and flower patterns below, trace 18 leaves, 18 reversed leaves, and four flowers onto the dull, nonwaxy side of the freezer paper. Cut out the shapes on the traced line to make freezer-paper templates. Use your favorite method and the green stripe and assorted plaids and stripes to prepare the leaves and flowers for appliqué.

4 Position the leaves along the vine, tucking one end under the vine and making sure the leaves are at least ¼" from the outer quilt edge. Pin a flower in each corner. Appliqué the leaves and flowers in place.

Finishing the Quilt

For more details on any finishing steps, visit ShopMartingale.com/HowtoQuilt for free downloadable information.

1 Layer the quilt top with batting and backing; baste the layers together.

2 Quilt by hand or machine. The quilt shown is machine quilted with an allover meandering design.

3 Use the black 2¼"-wide strips to make double-fold binding. Attach the binding to the quilt.

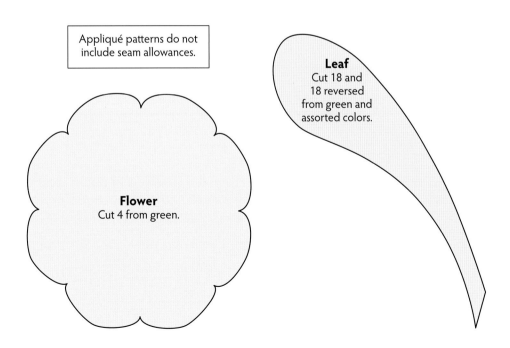

Appliqué patterns do not include seam allowances.

Flower
Cut 4 from green.

Leaf
Cut 18 and 18 reversed from green and assorted colors.

Flagstones

EVANDALE

Appliquéd wreath blocks surround a central eagle motif in this quilt reminiscent of yesteryear. The stars add movement and carry the navy into the sashing border that frames the eagle. The quilt is assembled in manageable rows. A gently scalloped border adds the final finish to this masterpiece.

❖◆❖

Materials

Yardage is based on 42"-wide fabric.

4¼ yards of cream print for blocks and outer border

1⅛ yards of navy stripe for eagle, inner border, and binding

½ yard of navy print for stars and inner border

1½ yards *total* of assorted red prints for stars and flowers

3 yards *total* of assorted green prints for leaves and stems

¼ yard *total* of assorted pink prints for flowers

4⅜ yards of fabric for backing

77" × 77" piece of batting

Seam sealant, such as Fray Block

Freezer paper

⅜" and ½" bias-tape makers

Water-soluble marker or chalk pencil

String

Cutting

All measurements include ¼" seam allowances.

From the cream print, cut:
- 5 strips, 20½" × 42"; crosscut into 9 squares, 20½" × 20½"
- 8 strips, 4½" × 42"

From the navy stripe, cut:
- 3 strips, 1½" × 42"

From the remainder of the navy stripe, cut *on the bias*:
- 2¼"-wide strips to total 290"

From the navy print, cut:
- 4 strips, 1½" × 42"

From the assorted green prints, cut a *total* of:
- 16 strips, 1" × 5"

From the remainder of the assorted green prints, cut *on the bias*:
- 8 strips, ⅞" × 36"
- 32 strips, ⅞" × 8"
- 1 strip, ⅞" × 17"
- 2 strips, ⅞" × 4"

FINISHED QUILT: 70½" × 70½"
FINISHED BLOCK: 20" × 20"

Appliquéd and quilted by Dawn Heese

Making the Wreath Blocks

Refer to "Appliqué Techniques" on page 91 as needed for more details. Use the photo on page 68 for placement guidance.

1 Seal the edges of each cream square using a seam sealant to prevent raveling and distortion during the appliqué process. Set aside one cream square for the Eagle block.

2 Fold the cream squares in half vertically and then horizontally; finger-press to establish centering creases. Tie the ends of a length of string to two water-soluble markers or chalk pencils so that the markers are 5¼" apart. Using the creases as a guide, place the tip of one marker in the center of a cream square. Keeping the string fully extended, draw a circle to make a placement guide for the wreath stem.

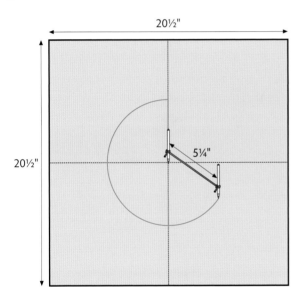

3 Using the ⅜" bias-tape maker and the green ⅞"-wide strips, prepare the 36"-long stems and 8"-long stems for appliqué. These stems are for the wreaths and corner flowers.

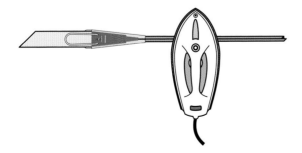

4 Repeat step 3 using the ½" bias-tape maker and the green 1" × 5" strips to prepare 16 stems for appliqué. These stems are for the center bouquets.

5 Using the patterns on page 73, trace the shapes the indicated number of times onto the dull, nonwaxy side of the freezer paper. Cut out the shapes on the traced line to make freezer-paper templates. Cut the number of pieces noted on the patterns from the fabrics indicated. Use your favorite method to prepare the shapes for appliqué.

6 Pin or baste a 36"-long stem on the marked circle. Position four corner stems, tucking them under the circular wreath stem. Pin the leaves and flowers in place, making sure the leaves are at least ½" from the outer edges of the square. For the center bouquet, layer the leaves and 6"-long stems first, followed by the blooms. Pin them in place. Appliqué the shapes in place. Repeat to make eight Wreath blocks measuring 20½" square, including seam allowances.

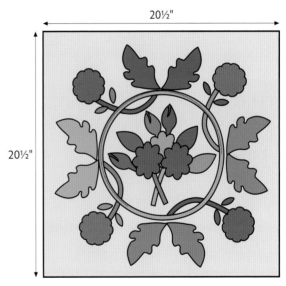

Wreath appliqué placement.
Make 8 blocks.

While this showstopping quilt is quite stunning, if you don't have the time to make the full quilt, consider making just three blocks for a hearty-sized runner, measuring 20½" × 60½". You can add borders to make it a bit larger. The runner would be quite the conversation piece on a dining table or sideboard, and it would look equally beautiful at the foot of your bed.

Making the Eagle Block

1 Referring to step 3 of "Making the Wreath Blocks," use the ⅜" bias-tape maker and the green ⅞"-wide strips to prepare one 17"-long stem and two 4"-long stems for appliqué.

2 Position the 17"-long stem on the prepared cream square set aside in step 1 of "Making the Wreath Blocks." Bend the stem into an arc and place it so the ends are about 4" from the sides of the square and will be sewn into the bottom seam allowance. The center of the stem should be 5¼" from the bottom edge of the square. Pin the stem in place. Pin the 4"-long stems in the center of the large stem and slightly overlap them.

3 Using the patterns on page 74 and pattern sheet 1, trace the shapes the indicated number of times onto the dull, nonwaxy side of the freezer paper. Cut out the shapes on the traced line to make freezer-paper templates. Cut the number of pieces noted on the pattern from the fabrics indicated. Use your favorite method to prepare the shapes for appliqué.

4 Center and pin the eagle on the curved stem. Add the leaves and stars around the eagle. Layer the branch under the eagle's beak. Appliqué the shapes in place.

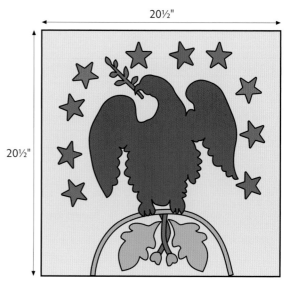

Eagle appliqué placement.
Make 1 block.

Assembling the Quilt Top

Press seam allowances in the directions indicated by the arrows.

1 Referring to the quilt assembly diagram below, lay out the blocks in three rows of three blocks each, placing the Eagle block in the center and noting the directions of each floral block. Sew the blocks into rows and then join the rows. The quilt top should measure 60½" square, including seam allowances.

2 Using the star patterns on page 75, trace eight large stars and eight medium stars onto the dull, nonwaxy side of the freezer paper. Cut out the shapes on the traced line to make freezer-paper templates. Cut the number of pieces noted on the patterns from the fabrics indicated. Use your favorite method to prepare the shapes for appliqué.

3 Referring to the photo on page 68, appliqué a navy star in the center of each red star. Appliqué the red/navy star on top of the seam intersection at each corner of the Eagle block. To manage the size of the quilt and make handling the bulk easier, roll and clip some of the extra fabric out of the way when stitching.

4 Join the navy stripe and navy print 1½"-wide strips randomly end to end. From the pieced strip, cut two 62½"-long strips and two 60½"-long strips. Sew the shorter strips to the left and right sides of the quilt center. Sew the longer strips to the top and bottom edges. The quilt top should measure 62½" square, including seam allowances.

5 Join the cream 4½"-wide strips end to end in pairs to make four strips. From the pieced strips, cut two 70½"-long strips and two 62½"-long

Quilt assembly

strips. Sew the shorter strips to the left and right sides of the quilt center. Sew the longer strips to the top and bottom edges. The quilt top should measure 70½" square.

6 In each corner, appliqué a red/navy star on top of the inner and outer borders.

Finishing the Quilt

For more details on any finishing steps, visit ShopMartingale.com/HowtoQuilt for free downloadable information.

1 Layer the quilt top with batting and backing; baste the layers together.

2 Quilt by hand or machine. The quilt shown is machine quilted with an outline stitch around the appliqués and stitched in the ditch along the borders. A meandering design is stitched in the background.

3 Trace the corner and side scallop patterns on pattern sheet 1 onto the dull, nonwaxy side of the freezer paper. Cut out the shapes on the marked line.

4 To mark the scallops in the outer border, align the straight edge of each template with the seamline. Using a water-soluble marker, trace the corner scallop in all four corners. Then trace the side scallops on each side of the quilt. The quilt may have shrunk a little after quilting, so the side scallops may not fit exactly. As you trace, adjust the length of the side scallops as needed to fit. Do *not* cut the scallops yet.

5 Use the navy stripe 2¼"-wide bias strips to make double-fold binding. Aligning the raw edges of the binding with the drawn scallops, sew the binding to the quilt. Start on the roundest part of a scallop and use a ¼" seam allowance. Stitch to the valley of the scallop. Stop with the needle down, pivot, and sew back out of the valley, taking care to avoid pleats.

6 Once the binding has been attached, trim the excess border and batting even with the edge of the binding. Turn the binding to the back of the quilt and stitch in place, easing as needed around the curves.

Center leaf
Cut 24 from green prints.

Appliqué patterns do not include seam allowances.

Side leaf
Cut 32 and 32 reversed from green prints.

Corner flower
Cut 32 from red prints.

Corner leaf 1
Cut 32 from green prints.

Corner leaf 2
Cut 32 from green prints.

Center flower
Cut 16 from red prints and 8 from pink prints.

Bud base
Cut 24 from green prints.

Bud
Cut 24 from red prints.

Evandale

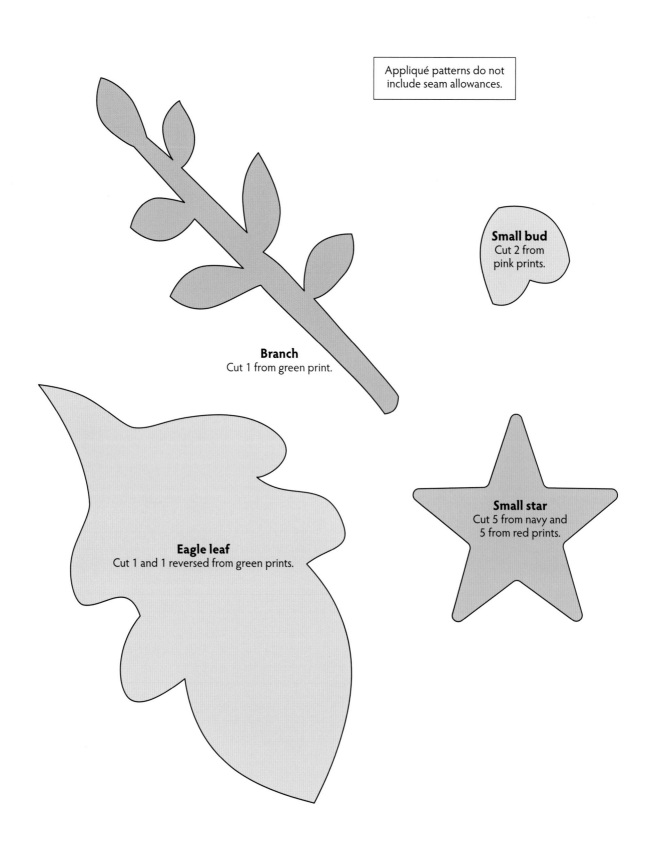

Appliqué patterns do not include seam allowances.

Small bud
Cut 2 from pink prints.

Branch
Cut 1 from green print.

Eagle leaf
Cut 1 and 1 reversed from green prints.

Small star
Cut 5 from navy and 5 from red prints.

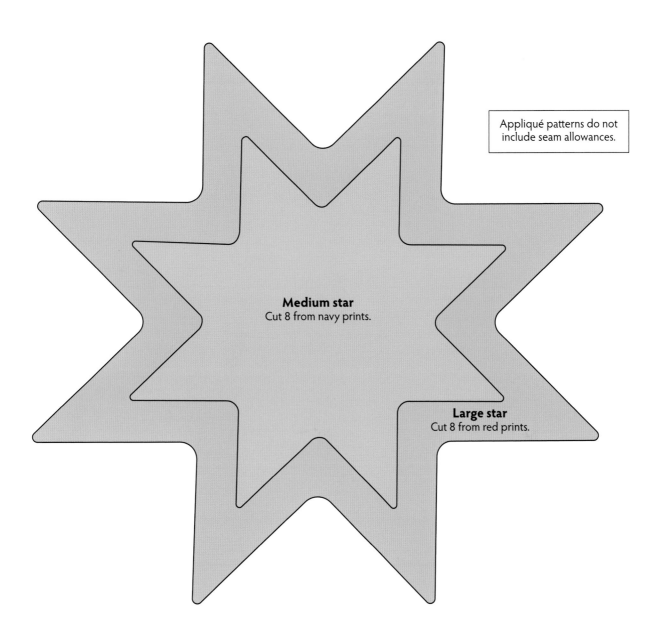

Appliqué patterns do not include seam allowances.

Medium star
Cut 8 from navy prints.

Large star
Cut 8 from red prints.

Evandale

75

HOPSCOTCH

*Pull out your fat quarters for this scrappy throw.
Quick-to-piece blocks make this a great weekend project.
The blocks are simple, but dressing them up with a
scalloped border adds a feminine finishing touch.*

Materials

*Yardage is based on 42"-wide fabric. Fat quarters measure
18" × 21".*

7 fat quarters *OR* 1¾ yards *total* of assorted light prints
  for block backgrounds

8 fat quarters *OR* 2⅞ yards *total* of assorted red, blue,
  pink, and taupe prints for blocks

⅓ yard of tan solid for sashing

⅓ yard of pink check for sashing

⅓ yard of red paisley A for border

⅜ yard of red paisley B for border

1 square, 8" × 8", of taupe print for sashing
  cornerstones

⅝ yard of red print for bias binding

3⅞ yards of fabric for backing

70" × 70" piece of batting

Freezer paper

Water-soluble marker

Cutting

All measurements include ¼" seam allowances.

From the assorted light prints, cut a *total* of:
- 81 squares, 3" × 3"
- 81 sets of 2 matching squares, 2⅝" × 2⅝" (162 total)

**From the assorted red, blue, pink, and taupe prints,
cut 81 matching sets of:**
- 4 pieces, 2¼" × 3" (324 total)
- 2 squares, 2⅝" × 2⅝" (162 total)

From the tan solid, cut:
- 12 strips, 1½" × 18½"

From the pink check, cut:
- 12 strips, 1½" × 18½"

From red paisley A, cut:
- 3 strips, 3" × 42"

From red paisley B, cut:
- 4 strips, 3" × 42"

From the taupe print, cut:
- 16 squares, 1½" × 1½"

From the red print, cut *on the bias*:
- 2¼"-wide strips to total 300"

FINISHED QUILT: 63½" × 63½"
FINISHED BLOCK: 18" × 18"

———————◆◆◆———————

Pieced and quilted by Dawn Heese

Making the Blocks

Press seam allowances in the directions indicated by the arrows.

1 Draw a diagonal line from corner to corner on the wrong side of the light 2⅝" squares. Layer a marked square on a red, blue, pink, or taupe square, right sides together. Sew ¼" from both sides of the drawn line. Cut the unit apart on the marked line to make two half-square-triangle units. Make 81 sets of four matching units measuring 2¼" square, including seam allowances.

Make 81 sets of
4 matching units,
2¼" × 2¼".

2 Lay out four half-square-triangle units, four matching print 2¼" × 3" pieces, and one matching light 3" square in three rows. Sew all the pieces into rows and then join the rows. Make 81 units measuring 6½" square, including seam allowances.

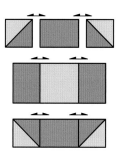 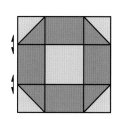

Make 81 units,
6½" × 6½".

3 Lay out nine units from step 2 in three rows as shown. Sew the units into rows and then join the rows. Make nine blocks measuring 18½" square, including seam allowances.

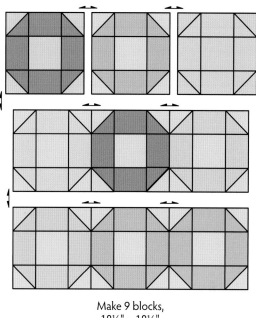

Make 9 blocks,
18½" × 18½".

Assembling the Quilt Top

1 Join three pink check strips and four taupe squares to make the top sashing row. Repeat to make the bottom sashing row.

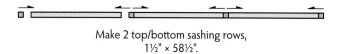

Make 2 top/bottom sashing rows,
1½" × 58½".

2 Join three tan strips and four taupe squares to make a center sashing row. Make two rows. The sashing rows should all measure 1½" × 58½", including seam allowances.

Make 2 center sashing rows,
1½" × 58½".

3 Join three blocks and two tan strips to make a row. Sew a pink check strip to each end of the row. Make three block rows measuring 18½" × 58½", including seam allowances.

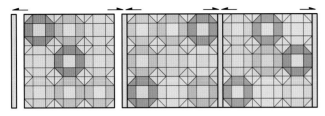

Make 3 block rows,
18½" × 58½".

4 Referring to the quilt assembly diagram below, join the block rows and center sashing rows. Sew the top and bottom sashing rows to the top and bottom edges. The quilt center should measure 58½" square, including seam allowances.

5 Join the three matching paisley 3"-wide strips end to end. From the pieced strip, cut two 58½"-long strips and sew them to the top and bottom of the quilt. Join the four matching paisley 3"-wide strips end to end. From the pieced strip, cut two 63½"-long strips and sew them to the left and right sides of the quilt. The quilt top should measure 63½" square.

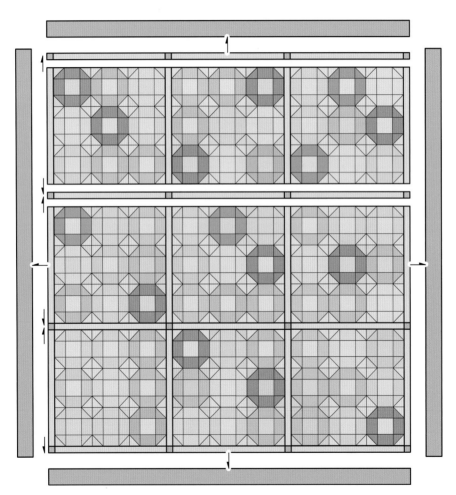

Quilt assembly

Finishing the Quilt

For more details on any finishing steps, visit ShopMartingale.com/HowtoQuilt for free downloadable information.

1 Layer the quilt top with batting and backing; baste the layers together.

2 Quilt by hand or machine. The quilt shown is machine quilted with an allover design of swirls.

3 Trace the corner and side scallop patterns on pages 82 and 83 onto the dull, nonwaxy side of the freezer paper. Cut out on the marked line.

4 To mark the scallops in the outer border, align the straight edge of each template with the seamline. Using a water-soluble marker, trace the corner scallop in all four corners. Trace the side scallop on each side of the quilt. The quilt may have shrunk a little after quilting, so the side scallops may not fit exactly. As you trace, adjust the length of the side scallop as needed to fit. Do *not* cut the scallops yet.

5 Use the red 2¼"-wide bias strips to make double-fold binding. Aligning the raw edges of the binding with the drawn scallops, sew the binding to the quilt. Start on the roundest part of a scallop and use a ¼" seam allowance. Stitch to the valley of the scallops. Stop with the needle down, pivot, and sew back out of the valley, taking care to avoid pleats.

6 Once the binding has been attached to the quilt, trim the excess border and batting even with the edge of the binding. Turn the binding to the back of the quilt and stitch in place, easing as needed around the curves.

Hopscotch

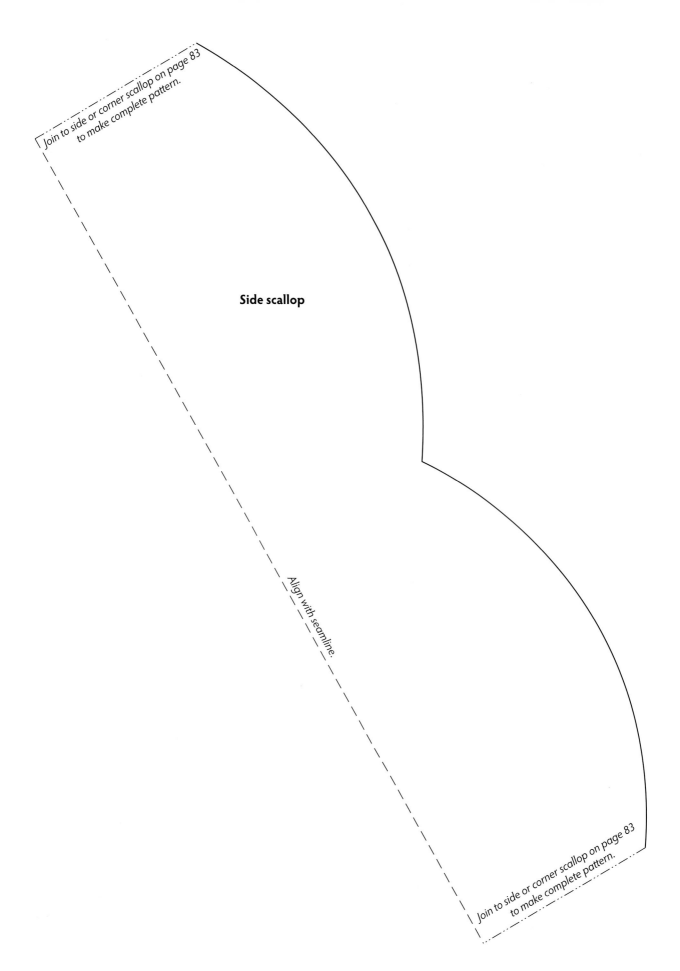

Side scallop

Join to side or corner scallop on page 83 to make complete pattern.

Align with seamline.

Join to side or corner scallop on page 83 to make complete pattern.

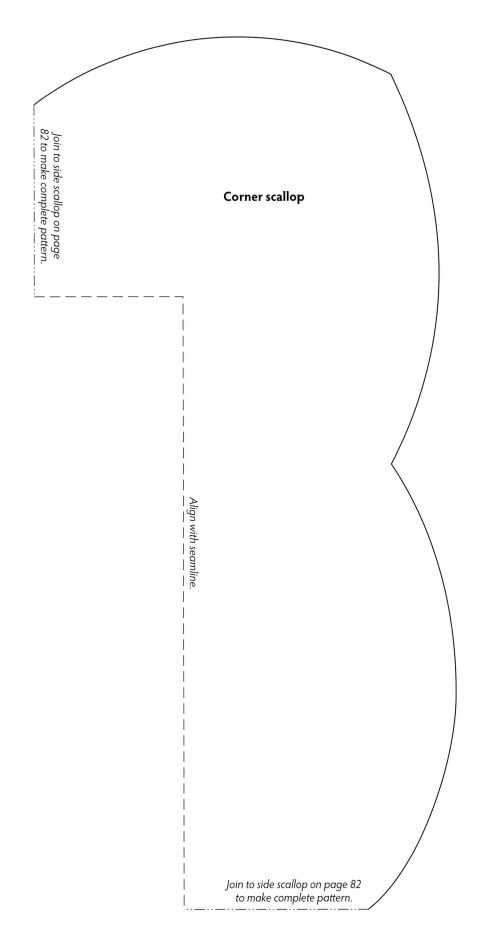

Corner scallop

Join to side scallop on page 82 to make complete pattern.

Align with seamline.

Join to side scallop on page 82 to make complete pattern.

Hopscotch

LATCHLEY RUNNER

This generously sized wool appliqué runner works perfectly at the foot of a bed or on a farmhouse table.

Materials

Cotton yardage is based on 42"-wide fabric.

COTTON

1⅜ yards of gray check for background and borders

1⅝ yards of fabric for backing

½ yard of burgundy woven stripe for bias binding

WOOL

15" × 16" piece of dark green for large star, leaves, and bud bases

12" × 18" piece of burgundy for flowers, petals, stars, and buds

10" × 15" piece of light green for flowers, flower bases, and scallops

4" × 12" piece of pink for flowers

4" × 7" piece of light orange for circles

ADDITIONAL MATERIALS

26" × 56" piece of batting

Seam sealant, such as Fray Block

Freezer paper

Pencil or water-soluble marker

Burgundy, dark green, light green, pink, and light orange 6-strand embroidery floss

Cutting

All measurements include ¼" seam allowances.

From the gray check, cut:

- 2 strips, 15½" × 42"; crosscut into 3 squares, 15½" × 15½"

- 4 strips, 2½" × 42"; crosscut *1 of the strips* into 2 strips, 2½" × 15½"

From the burgundy stripe, cut *on the bias*:

- 2¼"-wide strips to total 175"

FINISHED RUNNER: 19½" × 49½"
FINISHED BLOCK: 15" × 15"

Appliquéd and quilted by Dawn Heese

Making the Blocks

Refer to "Embroidery Stitches" on page 95. Use two strands of embroidery floss unless otherwise specified.

1 Seal the edges of the gray squares with seam sealant to prevent raveling and distortion during. Fold each square in half vertically and then horizontally. Finger-press centering creases. Unfold and then fold the square diagonally in both directions. Finger-press.

2 Referring to "Wool Appliqué" on page 93, trace the appliqué patterns on pages 88 and 89 and on pattern sheet 2 onto the dull, nonwaxy side of the freezer paper. Cut out the shapes directly on the line. Use the freezer-paper templates to cut the number of pieces noted on the patterns from the fabrics indicated.

3 Prepare three flower centers: layer the circle B, small, medium, and large flower pieces. Appliqué the shapes together.

4 For block A, using the creased lines as a guide, position the prepared flower in the center of a gray square. Place the dark green leaves on the diagonal creases, tucking the ends under the center flower.

Position the remaining shapes so they just touch each other. Using light orange floss, make a French knot in the center of each circle. Make straight stitches from the center to the outer edge of each circle to create spokes. Use matching floss to whipstitch around the perimeter of each shape. Repeat to make two A blocks measuring 15½" square, including seam allowances.

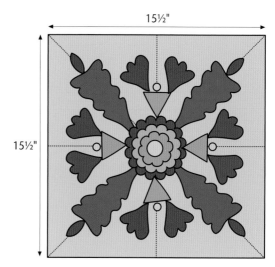

Block A appliqué placement.
Make 2 blocks.

5 For block B, using the diagram as a guide, position the large star in the center of a gray square. Place the prepared flower in the center of the star shape. Place the swags around the center star. Add a small bud to each point of the star and place a circle B on top of each star point to cover the end of the bud and swags. Center a burgundy star and a circle C in the space between the large star points and the swags. Using light orange floss, make a French knot in the center of each circle. Make straight stitches from the center to the outer edge of each circle to create spokes. Use matching floss to whipstitch around the perimeter of each shape. Make one B block measuring 15½" square, including seam allowances.

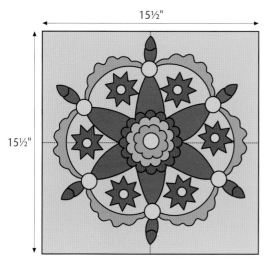

15½"

15½"

Block B appliqué placement.
Make 1 block.

Assembling the Table Runner

Press seam allowances in the directions indicated by the arrows.

1 Referring to the table-runner assembly diagram on page 88, join the blocks to make a row. The table-runner center should measure 15½" × 45½", including seam allowances.

2 Sew the gray 2½" × 15½" strips to the short ends of the table runner. Join the remaining gray 2½"-wide strips end to end. From the pieced strip, cut

two 49½"-long strips and sew them to the long sides of the table runner. The table runner should measure 19½" × 49½".

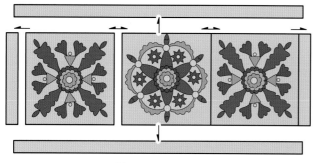

Table-runner assembly

Finishing the Runner

For more details on any finishing steps, visit ShopMartingale.com/HowtoQuilt for free downloadable information.

1 Layer the runner top with batting and backing; baste the layers together.

2 Quilt by hand or machine. The table runner shown is machine quilted with an allover meandering design in the background areas.

3 Trace the corner and side scallop patterns on page 90 and the center, right, and left long side scallops on pattern sheet 2 onto the dull, nonwaxy side of the freezer paper. Cut out the shapes on the marked line.

4 To mark the scallops in the border, align the straight edge of each template with the seamline. Using a water-soluble marker, trace the corner scallop in all four corners. Then trace the side scallop on each side of the runner. The runner may have shrunk a little after quilting, so the side scallops may not fit exactly. As you trace, adjust the length of the side scallop as needed to fit. Do *not* cut the scallops yet.

5 Use the burgundy 2¼"-wide bias strips to make double-fold binding. Aligning the raw edges of the bias binding with the drawn scallops, sew the binding to the runner. Start on the roundest part of a scallop and use a ¼" seam allowance. Stitch to the valley of the scallops. Stop with the needle down, pivot, and sew back out of the valley, avoiding pleats.

6 Once the binding has been attached to the runner, trim the excess border and batting even with the edge of the binding. Turn the binding to the back of the runner and stitch in place, easing as needed around the curves.

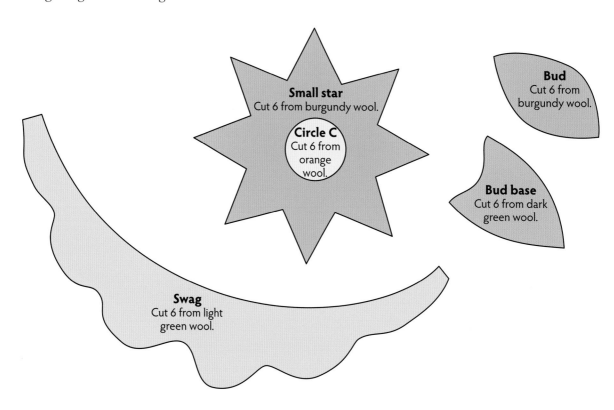

Plain & Fancy Quilts

88

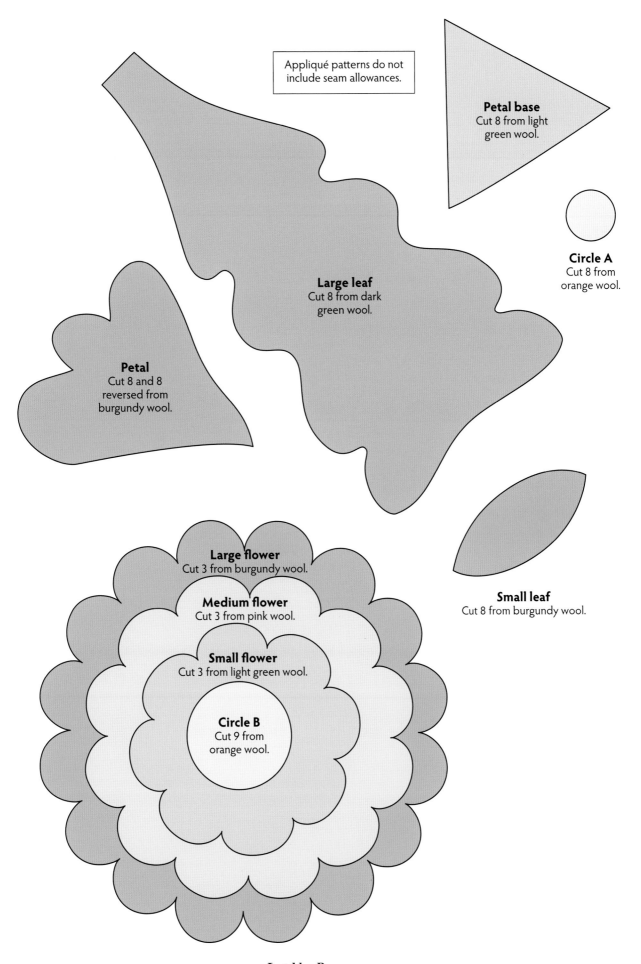

Appliqué patterns do not include seam allowances.

Petal base
Cut 8 from light green wool.

Circle A
Cut 8 from orange wool.

Large leaf
Cut 8 from dark green wool.

Petal
Cut 8 and 8 reversed from burgundy wool.

Small leaf
Cut 8 from burgundy wool.

Large flower
Cut 3 from burgundy wool.

Medium flower
Cut 3 from pink wool.

Small flower
Cut 3 from light green wool.

Circle B
Cut 9 from orange wool.

Latchley Runner

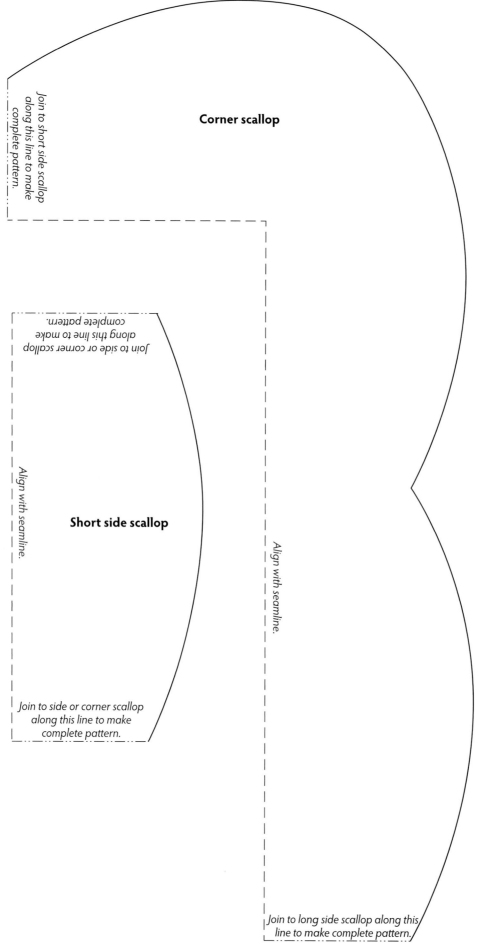

Corner scallop

Join to short side scallop along this line to make complete pattern.

Join to side or corner scallop along this line to make complete pattern.

Short side scallop

Align with seamline.

Align with seamline.

Join to side or corner scallop along this line to make complete pattern.

Join to long side scallop along this line to make complete pattern.

APPLIQUÉ TECHNIQUES

There are many ways to appliqué. My way is not the "right way," it's just the method that works best for me. I love to appliqué by hand rather than machine, but I don't like to spend my time on prep work. I prefer to get right to the stitching! Since I carry my appliqué with me practically everywhere I go, my method also requires very few supplies, so I don't have to tote a ton of them along.

Cotton Appliqué

Here are the basics for my appliqué technique.

1 Trace the pattern shapes on the dull side of a piece of freezer paper. Do not add a seam allowance to the patterns. Cut on the drawn line to make a freezer-paper template. The freezer paper will adhere to the fabric many times over using the heat of your iron, so if you need four of the same leaf, for example, you only need to cut one freezer-paper template and reuse it.

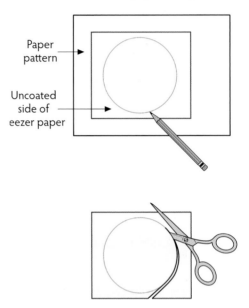

Paper pattern →

Uncoated side of eezer paper →

2 Iron the paper templates, shiny side down, to the right side of the fabric. Using a chalk pencil or water-soluble pen, trace around the template. Make sure the line is clearly visible as this will be the turning line. Cut out the fabric shape, adding an ⅛" to ¼" seam allowance around the template. Remove the freezer-paper template.

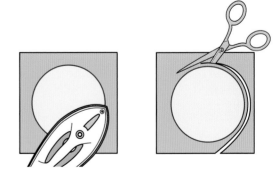

3 Cut a background square to the size indicated in the instructions. Seal the edges of the square with a seam sealant, such as Fray Block, to prevent raveling and distortion during the appliqué process. The seam sealant will dry clear and leave the edges of the fabric flexible.

4 Fold the background square in half vertically and horizontally and finger-press the folds. If appropriate for the design, unfold and then fold diagonally in both directions and finger-press. The fold lines will serve as a guide for placing the appliqué shapes on the background.

5 Pin or baste the appliqué shape in place on the background square. I use Clover appliqué pins as they have a thick shaft that keeps them from backing out of the piece. Their oval heads are also less likely to snag your thread.

6 Sew the appliqué shapes in the order that they are layered, starting with the bottommost pieces. Use the tip of your needle or a toothpick to turn under the seam allowance. To keep your curves smooth, turn under just what you need to stitch, don't turn under way ahead.

Wool Appliqué

I don't use fusible web for wool appliqué. I love the ease of stitching wool that hasn't been fused and prefer the look of the various textures you get without the glue.

1 Trace the patterns onto the dull, nonwaxy side of freezer paper, grouping shapes to be cut from the same color together. Roughly cut out the shape or group of shapes.

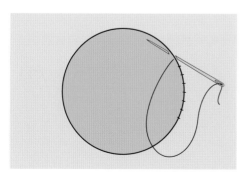

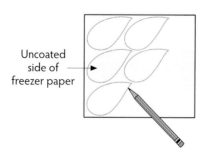

Uncoated side of freezer paper

Appliqué Techniques

2 Iron the freezer paper, shiny side down, to the wool. Cut out the shape on the drawn lines.

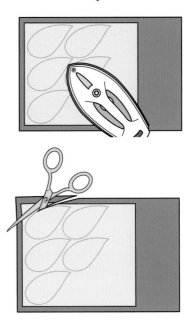

3 Staple or pin the shapes to the background. I prefer to staple them because they stay put and the staples don't leave behind holes as they might in lightweight cotton fabric. Whipstitch the appliqués in place using two strands of embroidery floss (see "Embroidery Stitches" on page 95).

EASY REVERSE

When working with wool, there's no need to make reverse templates for patterns that call for reversed pieces. Wool does not have a right or wrong side, so simply cut all the shapes the same and just flip the piece over to make a reversed shape when attaching it to the background.

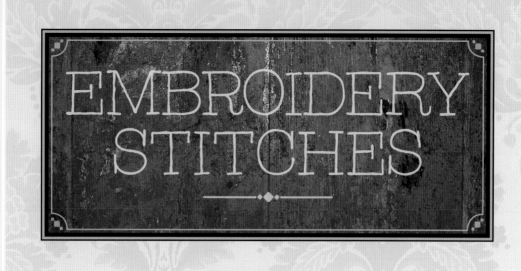

EMBROIDERY STITCHES

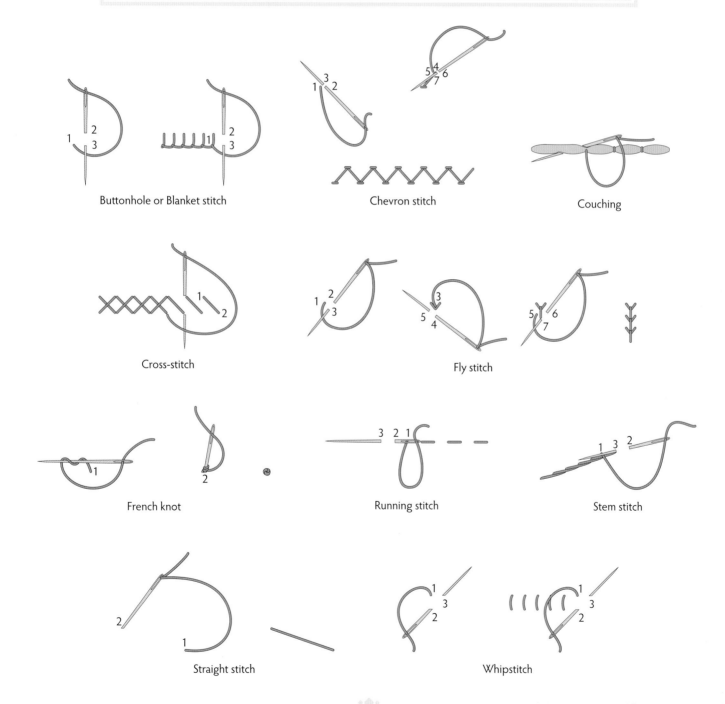

Buttonhole or Blanket stitch

Chevron stitch

Couching

Cross-stitch

Fly stitch

French knot

Running stitch

Stem stitch

Straight stitch

Whipstitch

ABOUT DAWN

Dawn Heese is an author, pattern designer, fabric designer, and award-winning quilter. She is a fourth-generation quilter, and grew up stitching from a young age. She began her career in the quilting industry with the publication of her first book in 2009. The following year, she started her design company, Linen Closet Designs, named for her grandmother's linen closet full of vintage quilts. Linen Closet Designs produces quilt and punch-needle patterns as well as fabric designs. Dawn's work is regularly featured in magazines in the United States and abroad. She teaches and presents trunk shows nationally and in France, sharing her love of appliqué and quilting. Dawn lives in Prairie Home, Missouri, with her significant other, Eric, in a 120-year-old farmhouse in the country. She has two grown sons and a grandson. Dawn also shares her home with a menagerie of dogs, cats, and two wily goats. This is her eighth book.